E.P.
2-5-86
$18.50

The Minimum Wage

Policy Studies Institute

The Minimum Wage

Frank Field

 Heinemann · London

Heineman Educational Books Ltd
22 Bedford Square, London WC1B 3HH
LONDON   EDINBURGH   MELBOURNE   AUCKLAND
HONG KONG   SINGAPORE   KUALA LUMPUR   NEW DELHI
IBADAN   NAIROBI   JOHANNESBURG
EXETER (NH)   KINGSTON   PORT OF SPAIN

ISBN 0 435 83300 6 cased

© Policy Studies Institute 1984
First published 1984

100265

Typeset by Inforum Ltd, Portsmouth
Printed in Great Britain by Biddles Ltd, Guildford, Surrey

Contents

Abbreviations — vii
Preface — ix

INTRODUCTION — 1

I. THE IMPORTANCE OF THE ISSUE

1. The Low Pay Issue — 7
   - The numbers of low paid — 8
   - Low pay and the wages council sector — 9
   - Decline in relative earnings — 10
   - Increase in tax burden — 12
   - Impact of inflation — 13

2. Developments since 1979 — 16
   - Tax changes — 16
   - Inflation — 17
   - Loss of protective machinery: Fair Wages Resolution — 18
   - Schedule 11 — 20
   - Talking down wages — 21

3. The Link with Poverty and Other Forms of Disadvantage — 25
   - Low pay and poverty — 25
   - Under-estimation of poverty — 27
   - Indirect cause of poverty – unemployment — 30
   - Sickness — 31
   - Old age — 33

4. The Poverty Trap and Incentives to Work — 37
   - Means-tested welfare — 37
   - Family Income Supplement — 38
   - Poverty trap — 39
   - Why-work syndrome — 42
   - SDP proposals — 45

II. A COMPREHENSIVE POLICY AGAINST LOW PAY

5. Child Benefit and the National Minimum Wage — 51
    The value of the national minimum wage — 51
    The national minimum wage and poverty — 54
    Children's needs — 57

6. What Costs and Who Benefits? — 60
    The costs — 60
    Employment consequences — 64
    Empirical results — 66

7. A Programme of Compensatory Measures — 71
    Employment effects — 71
    Inflationary effects — 74
    Incomes policy — 75
    Manpower and investment policy — 77

8. The Trade Unions' Response — 82
    Early period — 82
    Wages council sector — 84
    A voluntary approach again? — 88
    A policy on pay deals — 89

9. Fiscal Changes — 93
    Raising the tax threshold — 93
    A new social security tax — 98

10. Reform of the Equal Pay and Sex Discrimination Acts — 101
    Equal Pay Act — 101
    Sex Discrimination Act — 103
    Reform — 105

CONCLUSION — 108

Appendix 1. Calculations on the national minimum wage level — 110
Appendix 2. The importance of the child benefit scheme — 112

Index — 114

Abbreviations

CAC	Central Arbitration Committee
CB	Child Benefit
CBI	Confederation of British Industry
CIR	Commission on Industrial Relations
CPAG	Child Poverty Action Group
CPSA	Civil and Public Services Association
DE	Department of Employment
DEP	Department of Employment and Productivity
DHSS	Department of Health and Social Security
EOC	Equal Opportunities Commission
FES	Family Expenditure Survey
FIS	Family Income Supplement
GES	Government Economic Survey
GHS	General Household Survey
G & M	General, Municipal, Boilermakers and Allied Trades Union
IDS	Incomes Data Services
IEA	Institute of Economic Affairs
IFS	Institute for Fiscal Studies
LO	Swedish/Norwegian TUC
LPPI	Low Paid Price Index
LPU	Low Pay Unit
NAF	Norwegian Confederation of Employers
NBPI	National Board for Prices and Incomes
NES	New Earnings Survey
NMW	National Minimum Wage
NUPE	National Union of Public Employees
OECD	Organisation for Economic Co-operation and Development
OPCS	Office of Population, Census and Surveys
PSI	Policy Studies Institute
RPI	Retail Price Index
SDP	Social Democratic Party
SEG	Socio-Economic Group
SMIC	Minimum Inter-Occupational Incremental Wage (French minimum wage)

TGWU/T & G Transport & General Workers Union
TUC   Trades Union Congress

Preface

I wish to record my thanks to a large number of people who have helped in producing this book. The typing has been shared between Joanne Laver, at the Policy Studies Institute, and Joan Hammell, who is my secretary at the House of Commons. Both Joanne and Joan have cheerfully and efficiently tackled this task on top of all their other duties. I am particularly grateful to Richard Cracknell who undertook many of the calculations needed for this book and to Celia Nield who read through chapter 10. I also wish to thank Rob Clements, Julia Lourie, and Robert Twigger who supplied me with information, and the House of Commons Library for its efficient services. I also wish to record my thanks to Joan Brown, Sir Charles Carter, John Pinder and Barbara Rodgers who commented on the draft text, to Paul Ormerod who read through Chapter 6, to Neil McIlwraith who read through all the chapters and to Margaret Cornell for editing the manuscript and for compiling the index. While I am grateful to all these individuals, I, alone, am responsible for the opinions and interpretations to be found on the following pages.

Birkenhead
December 1983   Frank Field

Introduction

This book has its roots in the Policy Studies Institute's international seminar on minimum wages which took place in December 1982. At that conference, the papers of which have been published by PSI (Frank Field (ed.), *Policies Against Low Pay: the International Perspective*, PSI, 1984), I argued against those delegates who believed low wages to be an unimportant cause of poverty, and particularly family poverty. It was these delegates who, arguing from such a premise, stressed the irrelevance of a minimum wage strategy. Others asserted that the minimum wage debate was essentially about guaranteeing every worker – irrespective of family circumstance – a decent wage. It was not seen by them as concerned only or primarily as a means of tackling poverty; more was involved. The minimum wage campaign was about imposing upon the labour market the moral value that every worker had the right to a decent reward.

While supporting this argument, I was, at the same time, unhappy with the line taken by some of those supporting a national minimum wage (NMW) of two-thirds average earnings. A NMW at this level would have important economic repercussions, particularly on employment levels, and there seemed to be a tendency to play down such effects. In addition, my belief at that time was that, if the primary aim was to break the link between earnings and poverty, a NMW could be set at a lower level than was being proposed.

After the conference I looked more closely at two sets of figures. The first was the Family Expenditure Survey (FES) data on the composition of poor households. This showed the importance of low pay as a cause of poverty; almost a third of those who were below pensionable age and were found to be poor in 1979 were living in households where the main income was the weekly wage packet. I also re-worked the data on the income a wage earner would need if his (or her) take-home pay was to be equal to his supplementary benefit entitlement, in order to judge the level at which a NMW would need to be set if it were to become an effective instrument against family poverty. (The calculations are set out in Appendix 1.) Far from setting a minimum wage at a lower level, these results showed the need substantially to increase the minimum wage target level from £90.00 to £102.00 a week (in 1983).

Another major consequence followed from seeing a NMW primarily in terms of combatting family poverty. The role of child benefit not only enters the discussions, but moves towards the centre of them. Yet this was one aspect almost totally ignored at PSI's conference; (Barbara Rodgers' contribution to the discussion was a noble exception). As Chapter 5 of this book shows, a fully developed child benefit system has a dramatic effect on the level at which a NMW needs to be pitched.

All these three points – low pay as a major cause of poverty, a NMW seen primarily in terms of combatting family poverty, and the major impact of a fully developed child benefit scheme on the level of a minimum wage – are controversial (particularly the first two) and the arguments for them need to be developed more fully. This book is therefore an attempt to meet the objections which will be made to them, while at the same time setting out fully the case for a minimum wage. It also examines the range of other policies which need to accompany this strategy.

There is a further reason why the case for a NMW, and its likely economic consequences, should be given careful scrutiny. Trade union attitudes to this issue are changing, and so too are views within the Labour Party. The Liberal Party has long campaigned for a NMW. Of the non-conservative parties, only the SDP remains critical. There is a likelihood that centre-left radicals may wish to move quickly on this front should they form a majority in the next Parliament. The hope is that the two publications resulting from the PSI conference, and the follow-up work planned at the Institute, will help settle the question as to whether a NMW offers a real prospect of positive change for poorer people, or whether it is a dangerous blind alley to be avoided at all costs.

The case for a NMW strategy is developed in the following way. Section I looks at the situation as it is at present. The first two chapters examine what is known about the numbers of the low-paid, what has happened to their relative living standards, and how their already meagre living standards have been eroded by fiscal changes in inflation. Chapter 3 tries to assess the importance of low pay as both a direct and indirect cause of poverty. Chapter 4 examines the basis of the poverty trap and the incentives-to-work question.

The second section begins the argument for a comprehensive policy aimed at improving the living standards of low-paid workers. Chapter 5 explains why the introduction of a NMW needs to be linked to a fully developed child benefit scheme. It also sets out the calculations of the level at which a NMW must be set, together with child benefit, if it is to break the link between earnings and poverty. The next chapter looks at the costs and benefits of a minimum wage. This is followed in Chapter 7 by a discussion on the range of measures which needs to accompany a NMW if the employment and inflationary consequences associated with its introduction are to be countered. It is assumed throughout this book that a NMW will need to be given a statutory basis. Chapter 8 looks at what the trade unions will need to propose if there is to be a serious discussion on bringing in a NMW through collective bargaining only. And because the aim of a NMW strategy is to raise the living standards of the low-paid, Chapter 9 reviews the line direct tax reforms need to take if any increase in wages resulting from a NMW is not to be eaten away by rises in the tax burden. The final chapter argues the case for further reforms of the Equal Pay and Sex Discrimination Acts.

I
THE IMPORTANCE OF THE ISSUE

Low pay is once again moving up the political agenda. While the Low Pay Unit, which has campaigned ceaselessly on this issue since its foundation in 1974, can claim part of the credit, other forces have also been at work. Throughout the 1960s and 1970s a minority of the trade union movement campaigned, both as unions and within the TUC, to improve the position of low-paid workers (see chapter 8). With the rapid increase in unemployment, particularly since 1980, a more general trade union interest has again begun to focus on ways of limiting the effect of rising unemployment on wage levels. Part of this concern has shown itself in discussions on how to improve the position of the low-paid. In addition, the public debate has been fuelled by research findings from universities, independent research institutes, and the Government itself on the extent of low pay and on the living standards of lower paid workers. This section begins by looking at the size of the problem and what has been happening to the relative earnings of low-paid workers. It goes on to examine the extent to which increased taxation and the differential impact of inflation have affected the living standards of the low-paid compared with other groups in the workforce. The discussion then turns to examine the link between low pay and poverty, and reviews the debate on what has become known as the 'incentives to work' issue.

1 The Low-Pay Issue

The numbers of low-paid

Papers at the PSI Conference considered the different ways low pay has been defined in this country[1]. Because each of these definitions is looked at in more detail in Chapter 5, we need only list what these definitions are. The approach adopted by the National Board for Prices and Incomes (NBPI) was to look on those earning less than the lowest decile as falling in the category of low pay. Trade unions viewed the low-paid as those earning below the supplementary benefit entitlement for a two-child family. The much more common view now is for those earning less than two-thirds average earnings to be put into the category of low-paid. The most recent definition comes from the European Social Charter, and this is the one used here in order to illustrate the dimensions of the low-pay problem in Great Britain. But whatever definition is adopted it is important at the outset to make a distinction between low pay and poverty. Throughout this book poverty is defined as the current supplementary benefit income which Parliament lays down for those who are unable to work. Many people earning low wages will also be poor, but that is not true of every low-paid worker. The overlap between low pay and poverty is examined in more detail in Chapter 3.

The European Social Charter asserts a worker's 'right to a fair remuneration' and requires that governments should 'recognise the right of workers to a remuneration such as will give them and their families a decent standard of living'. This objective could be met, the committee of experts drawing up the Charter asserted, at a wage of 68 per cent of the national average wage, and they urged that this level should be viewed as 'a decency threshold'.[2] Using this 'decency threshold' and applying it to the distribution of earnings in the UK, what does it tell us about the number of wage earners at the lower end of the income scale?

The number of workers earning below this threshold of 68 per cent of average earnings (or the nearest cut-off point to this level in the New Earnings Survey (NES) is presented in Table 1.1. It is based on the

---

[1] See Liz Bisset and Emma MacLennan, 'Britain's minimum wage system' in Frank Field (ed.) *Policies Against Low Pay* (PSI, 1984).

[2] For more details on this, see Steve Winyard, *Fair Remuneration*, Low Pay Report 11, 1982.

Table 1.1 *Estimated numbers earning below the Committee of Experts low pay threshold, 1974–82*

Year and threshold	NES cut-off point	Men 21 and over Manual (million)	Men 21 and over Non-manual (million)	Total (million)	Women 18 and over Manual (million)	Women 18 and over Non-manual (million)	Total (million)	Grand Total (Men and women) (million)	% of all employed
1974 (£28.32)	£28(a)	0.7	0.3	0.9	1.6	2.1	3.5	4.5	26
1975 (£36.73)	£37	0.7	0.3	1.1	1.3	1.9	3.1	4.2	25
1976 (£43.65)	£44(a)	0.7	0.3	1.1	1.1	1.8	2.8	3.9	24
1977 (£47.76)	£48(a)	0.7	0.3	1.0	1.1	1.7	2.7	3.7	22
1978 (£53.79)	£54(a)	0.8	0.3	1.1	1.1	1.8	2.9	4.0	24
1979 (£60.90)	£60	0.7	0.3	0.9	1.1	1.7	2.8	3.7	22
1980 (£74.93)	£75	0.8	0.3	1.1	1.0	1.8	2.8	4.0	24
1981 (£84.90)	£80	0.9	0.3	1.2	1.0	1.7	2.6	3.8	25
1982 (£92.80)	£93(a)	0.9	0.3	1.2	1.0	1.7	2.6	3.8	25

Note: Sub-totals are rounded and may not therefore equal the sum totals.
(a) Numbers estimated by linear interpolation.
Sources: *New Earnings Survey*: Part A 1974–1981 Tables 22–23
Part B 1982 Tables 29, 37, 38.

average earnings of all full-time men aged 21 and over and women aged 18 and over, in all industries and services, but excluding those whose pay was affected by absence from work. It details the numbers of male and female workers earning below this level for each year since 1974 and classifies them according to whether they were manual or non-manual workers. It also gives the total number of workers earning below this 'decency threshold' and as a percentage of all workers employed.

What stands out most clearly from Table 1.1 is the number of workers earning below the 'decency threshold'. While it is true that the total numbers earning less than 68 per cent of average earnings have fallen from 4.5 million in 1974 to 3.8 million in 1982, these totals, once expressed as a percentage of all those employed, stubbornly remain around the 25 per cent mark.[3]

Low pay and the wages council sector

In Chapter 6 we shall see that low-paid female workers are concentrated in a fairly narrow band of industries. Some, but not all, of these industries make up what is known as the wages council sector. As we saw in Chapter 1 of the papers from the PSI Conference[4], today's Wages Councils have their roots in what were originally called 'trades boards', the first four of which were established by the 1909 Act. The system was extended after the First World War and they were renamed 'Wages Councils' in 1945. Despite the fact that these councils have the power to lay down minimum rates of remuneration, many workers covered by the wages council machinery are low paid. Just how sizeable this total is can be seen from Table 1.2.

These data come from the NES and, if they are weighted as a proportion of the total NES population, we find that 70.6 per cent of all wages council workers are low paid. The Wages Inspectorate estimate 2,734,800 people to be employed in this sector; if this figure is correct, then a total of 1,930,800 wages council workers are low paid. But there are a number of reasons to suggest that this is an under-estimate. The view of the Society of Civil and Public Servants is that the Wages Inspectorate under-estimates by around 20 per cent the number of establishments covered by wages orders. Moreover, the NES figure excludes male workers aged under 21 and women workers aged under

---

[3] Too much should not be made of the fact that the number of low-paid men has grown from 900,000 to 1,200,000 in the period since 1974. The total number of low-paid men in any one category is small and the increase could be accounted for in the rounding-up process which has had to be applied to each category.

[4] *Policies Against Low Pay, op. cit.*

Table 1.2 *Workers earning below £2.25 an hour in the wages council sector, 1981*

	% of wages council workers
Full-time manual men	39.9
Full-time non-manual men	24.2
Full-time manual women	89.1
Full-time non-manual women	82.7
Part-time women	93.0

Source: Data calculated by Dominic Byrne of the Low Pay Unit from the *New Earnings Survey*.

18, and also part-time workers earning below the national insurance threshold.

How does the number of low-paid workers in the wages council sector compare with the rest of the economy? Taking the same cut-off point of £2.25 an hour as a low-pay yardstick, we find that, while 70 per cent of wages council workers earn less than this sum, the total falls to a little over 25 per cent for the total economy. So, while Wages Councils cover less than 14 per cent of the workforce, they account for over 37 per cent of all low-paid workers. The vulnerability of these workers needs to be kept in mind in the following chapter, where we examine the present Government's attitude and actions towards the wages council system since 1979.

Decline in relative earnings

Poverty has always been defined in Britain in relative terms.[5] As well as looking at the number of low-paid, it is also important to look at the dispersion of earnings, and particularly the relation of the lowest decile. These data are presented in Table 1.3.

Figures for the dispersion of weekly earnings of male manual workers exist for as far back as 1886. In that year the wages paid to the lowest decile stood at 68 per cent of median earnings. Data were again collected in 1906 and the value of the lowest decile's wages, as compared against the median, fell to 66.5 per cent – the lowest point ever recorded in any of the surveys. Earnings surveys have been conducted annually since 1963. The results for all these survey years show that the value of the pay of the lowest decile never fell below 67.3 per cent of median earnings, and never rose above 71.6 per cent: a dispersion of

---

[5] See Frank Field, *Poverty and Politics* (Heinemann, 1982), Chap. 8, which shows this to have been Seebohm Rowntree's approach too, notwithstanding political and academic assertions to the contrary.

Table 1.3 *Lowest decile of gross weekly earnings as a percentage of median gross weekly earnings, results from 1866 onwards*

Year	Manual men Lowest decile as percentage of median	Manual women Lowest decile as percentage of median
1886	68.6	—
1906	66.5	—
1938	67.7	64.3
1960	70.6	72.0
1963	70.7	68.5
1964	71.6	65.1
1965	69.7	66.5
1966	68.6	66.3
1967	69.8	66.1
1968	67.3	71.1
1970	67.3	69.0
1971	68.2	70.2
1972	67.6	68.9
1973	67.3	69.2
1974	68.6	69.1
1975	69.2	68.4
1976	70.2	67.8
1977	70.6	70.3
1978	69.4	70.8
1979	68.3	70.4
1980	68.4	70.5
1981	69.7	69.6
1982	68.3	69.2

Source: *British Labour Statistics, Historical Abstract*, (HMSO, 1971), table 79, for years up to 1968; subsequent years from the NES.

4 percentage points. Indeed, as the Department of Employment's *Gazette* for October 1981 recalled, the dispersion of manual men's earnings 'has changed little, particularly at the lower end, over the period from 1886 to the present day' (p. 446).

The survey results on women workers, which began in 1938, show a much wider dispersion. The relative value of the lowest decile's earnings stood at its lowest point in 1938, when it was recorded at 64.3 per cent of median earnings. Data were again collected in 1960, and the results recorded the highest relative point for the poorest 10 per cent of manual women earners: an average of 72 per cent of median earnings. In most of the following years, the value fell, but it rose again to 70.8 per cent in 1978. Since then the NES results have shown a continual decline, and in 1982 the earnings of the lowest decile stood at 69.2 per cent of median earnings.

In a period of rising unemployment, and at a time when unemployment has fallen most heavily on those with lowest earnings, it might have been expected that the relative earnings of the low-paid still in work would have risen in relation to average earnings, but this has not happened. It would appear that rising unemployment has had a general effect in helping to hold down wages; and, perhaps more importantly, as low-paid workers become unemployed, other workers have stepped into their shoes.

Increase in tax burden

Not only have the numbers of low-paid remained stubbornly high, and not only has there been a marked decline in the relative earnings of the lowest paid, but there is also evidence that the living standards of this group have risen less fast than those of other groups of workers. This has been brought about by a disproportionate increase in their tax burden, and the impact of a higher rate of inflation than that recorded by the retail price index.

Over the past thirty years the tax burden has moved in two directions – both vertically and horizontally. The reason for this is twofold. In the first place, there has been a major erosion of the income-tax base, brought about by the policies of successive governments in exempting large tracts of personal income from tax by the granting and revaluing of a hundred or so tax allowances. These allowances range from the personal allowances to the tax concessions granted to people saving by way of a pension scheme or the mortgage interest relief subsidy to those buying their own homes. As many of these tax allowances or, as they should more correctly be called, tax benefits have grown in real terms over the years, the tax base has correspondingly shrunk. Secondly, and compounding this trend, there has been the willingness of governments to meet an ever-increasing range of expenditure. The result of these two trends has been the lowering of the tax threshold, but it has not fallen equally for all types of taxpayers.

While more and more people have been pulled into tax, the most hard-hit group has been those with children. The tax threshold for a taxpayer with two children stood at a fraction under average earnings (95.9 per cent) in 1955. But while income tax was levied at around average earnings for this family, the first bands of income attracted tax at only 8.75 pence in the pound. In 1955, a taxpayer with two children did not begin to pay income tax at the basic or standard rate until his or her earnings reached 178 per cent of average earnings. Since 1955 not only has the tax threshold continued to fall but, with the phasing-out of the reduced rates of tax, taxpayers have begun to pay the basic rate of tax at an ever lower level of income. The last remaining reduced band of tax was abolished in the 1969 budget and was not re-introduced until 1978, to be abolished again the following year. In 1982, a two-child family began to pay tax at 33.8 per cent of average earnings, and tax is paid immediately at the standard rate of 30p in the pound. On top of this a national insurance contribution was collected on all income at a rate of 8.75p in the pound; only those earning less than £29.40 a week were exempt from payment.

The tax threshold has also fallen for a single person, but at nowhere near the rate of a taxpayer with children. In 1955 the tax threshold for a single person, expressed as a percentage of average male earnings, stood at 32.9 per cent, and, as with other taxpayers, the tax rate on the first £1.00 of taxable income stood at 8.75 pence. By 1982 the threshold had fallen to 21.6 per cent of average male earnings and, as with other taxpayers, tax was immediately levied at 30 per cent.

Impact of inflation

Whilst tax and national insurance contributions determine the level of net pay, the rate of inflation determines the level of real living standards between one pay settlement and the next. It is therefore important to look at how the rate of inflation is measured and to try to gauge the extent to which it has varied according to the income level of the consumer.

The most commonly accepted measurement of the rate of inflation in this country is the retail price index. Obviously, the range of goods and services making up the index will affect its accuracy; so too will the weightings given to each of these different items of expenditure. Poorer people spend a larger proportion of their incomes on basic necessities, such as fuel, food and housing, than do other groups of the population. Thus if the rise in the cost of these items is greater than the general rise in prices, an index relating to an average family will underestimate the true cost of living for those on lower incomes.

In evidence to the Royal Commission on the Distribution of Income and Wealth, David Piachaud considered the differential impact of inflation during the period 1956–74. Up to 1966, his calculations showed that prices had risen by almost 11 percentage points more for those on incomes 5 percentage points from the bottom of the income scale than for those on incomes 5 percentage points from the top. The differential impact of inflation then lessened in the years between 1966 and 1971 but the difference in rises in the cost of living for rich and poor began to diverge once again during the 1971–4 period. During these years the richest 5 per cent experienced an increase in the cost of living of around 31 per cent, whereas the cost of living for the poorest 5 per cent rose by 35 per cent. Piachaud calculated that, over the whole period from 1956 to 1974, prices had increased by 26 percentage points more for those living at the bottom 5 percentage points in the income distribution, and by almost 31 percentage points more than households living on incomes 5 percentage points from the top of the incomes scale.[6]

What has been the record since 1974? We have seen that one criticism of the RPI has been that at various periods the baskets of goods and services from which the calculations are made represent a pattern of expenditure which has long ceased to mirror that of working families. A more recent criticism comes from Professor Muellbauer who highlights the fact that the RPI represents a household living on an income between 60 and 80 per cent up the income scale; just where the family comes on the scale depends on the family size.[7] As a consequence the Low Pay Unit decided to construct a Low Paid Price Index (LPPI) based on the spending patterns of the poorest 10 per cent of wage earners. Unfortunately information is not available from the Family Expenditure Survey on expenditure patterns by incomes of households where the head of the household is in employment. The LPU therefore decided to base its index on the FES data of all households living around or below the lowest decile of earnings.[8] What level of inflation has this index recorded?

Over the period March 1974 to March 1979 (which spans the life of the Wilson and Callaghan administrations) the LPPI recorded an increase of 211 per cent. This compares with a rise of 205.3 per cent in the RPI. In other words, prices rose faster during this period for those on lower incomes than for those whose cost of living is accurately measured by the RPI, namely by 5.7 percentage points, an extra rise in prices equivalent to the total weekly purchases of bread and fresh milk of a low-income family.

Conclusion

This chapter has used the European Social Charter's definition of low pay to show just how numerous are today's low paid: around 25 percent of the workforce. Moreover, it appears that the relative living standards of the low-paid have suffered a long-term decline: the earnings of the

[6] David Piachaud, *Prices and the distribution of incomes. Evidence submitted to the Royal Commission on the distribution of Income and Wealth*. (HMSO, December 1976).

[7] J. Muellbauer, *The Cost of Living* (Mimeographed, 1976).

[8] For further details on these calculations see the CPSA/Low Pay Unit price index note, 'Methods of calculations' n.d.).

lowest decile have fallen compared with median earnings, and the low-paid have been faced with a more rapidly rising tax bill and a higher rate of inflation than those experienced by other groups. We now turn to look at changes since 1979 before going on to examine the link between low pay and poverty and its overlap with other forms of disadvantage.

2 Developments since 1979

This chapter considers the extent to which the trends outlined in Chapter 1 have been countered or exacerbated since 1979. It looks at tax changes over the past four years and the extent to which there is still a difference in the rate of inflation experienced by low-paid workers compared with other groups of the population. It then goes on to review the changes the Government has made to the Fair Wages Resolution and to what is called 'Schedule 11'. The last section examines government policies about the level of wage settlements for the low-paid in general, and its attitude to the settlements in the wages councils sector in particular.

Tax changes

Since 1979 the level of taxation has increased for practically all taxpayers, and particularly for those on low pay as well as those with children. Table 2.1 contains the results of an analysis of the changes in income tax and national insurance contributions, comparing the position in the financial year 1978/79 with that of 1982/83.

Table 2.1 *Increase in the proportion of income taken in tax and national insurance contributions 1978/79 to 1982/83 (percentage points)*

	Single person	Married couple both working	Married couple plus 2 children (a)
50% average earnings	+3.8	+3.7	+6.3
75% average earnings	+2.4	+5.3	+4.1
100% average earnings	+1.5	+4.4	+2.9
200% average earnings	+0.9	+1.9	+1.6
500% average earnings	−6.3	−0.3	−5.3

Note: (a) treats child benefit as income.
Source: *House of Commons Hansard*, 17 March 1983, and House of Commons Library.

This analysis confirms that all household types earning twice average earnings and less have experienced an increase in taxation. It also shows that, whatever the income level chosen, taxes have increased fastest for those on the lowest incomes – and faster still if low income is combined with family responsibilities. Whereas a single person earning twice average earnings, for example, has seen his tax load increase as a percentage of his earnings by 0.9 per cent, the increase for a single person on two-thirds average earnings has been 2.4 per cent. For similarly placed taxpayers with two children, the increases are 1.6 and 4.1 per cent respectively. The position of those on half average earnings shows an even larger increase in the proportion of their income going in taxation in 1982/83 compared with 1978/79. For a single person, the increase has been 3.8 per cent; for a married couple with two children, 6.3 per cent. It is only at higher levels of income, illustrated in Table 2.1 at five times average earnings, that the Government has fulfilled its 1979 election commitment to reduce taxation, but even here the reduction has been greatest for childless taxpayers.

Inflation

The RPI rose by 54.7 per cent from May 1979 to May 1983, equivalent to an annual average increase of 11.5 per cent. This period has seen frequent variations in the differential impact of inflation. The LPPI shows that price increases for the lower paid during the early months of 1979 were about the same as those being experienced by the rest of the population. The position changed, however, after the 1979 budget which brought about a sharp increase in VAT, only to be followed by the rise in mortgage interest rates later in the year. According to the LPPI calculations, by the Spring of 1980, inflation for higher-income groups was running at just over 2 percentage points above that of low-income groups. By the middle of 1980, the rise in living costs for those on low incomes was again matching that for high income earners and by the beginning of 1981 the inflation rate for the poor was 2 percentage points greater than that for more affluent households. During 1981, when the RPI recorded an increase of around 12 per cent, the cost of living of low-income households was rising at between 14 and 15 per cent.

Comparing the beginning of 1980 with the end of 1981, the cost of living for the poorest households had risen by almost 30 per cent. The official Retail Price Index, by contrast, recorded an increase of less than 26 per cent over this two-year period.[1]

In other words, despite a period when the inflation rate has been falling, prices have still been rising faster for low-income consumers than for those higher up the income scale.

This differential impact of inflation was maintained through the remainder of the Thatcher Government's first administration. By the time of the 1983 General Election, the cost of living of the low-paid had

---

[1] Bill Smith, *Prices and the Poor*, Low Pay Report, n.d., p. 4.

increased by 57.6 per cent, which was nearly 4 percentage points above the rate of inflation measured by the RPI; an additional rise in prices equivalent to a low-income family's weekly purchase of eggs, bread and footwear. The Low Paid Price Indexes, published at the end of a Parliament, show that the low-paid continued to be hit harder by inflation because of disproportionate price increases of key commodities. Fuel costs, for instance, increased by 11.8 per cent in the twelve months up to April 1983; gas prices rose by 19 per cent. And while those paying rents experienced a 6 per cent increase in the twelve months up to April 1983 and a 4–5 per cent increase between March and April 1983 alone, those with mortgages saw a 19 per cent reduction in their housing costs.

Loss of protective machinery: Fair Wages Resolution

Since 1979 two forms of protection for the low-paid (and for employers who were safeguarded against competition based on wage-cutting) have been abolished: the Fair Wages Resolution and Schedule 11. The history of the Fair Wages Resolution goes back to 1891 when the House of Commons gave its unanimous approval to the Resolution as a means of combatting 'the evils recently disclosed before the Sweating Committee'. The Resolution laid down that employers tendering for public contracts should pay the wages generally accepted in the trade for similar work.

The weakness of the 1891 Resolution, and its reform in 1909, has been reported upon elsewhere.[2] What is important to note here is how this protective machinery was extended to different parts of the labour market. All the early reforms centred on extending the remit of the Resolution within the public sector. During the Second World War it was extended to the private sector, but until the passing of Schedule 11 of the 1975 Employment Protection Act, wage comparisons in the private sector were restricted to the rates of pay and terms and conditions of employment established by a collective agreement.[3] Schedule 11 made a major change, in that it allowed claims to be based on comparisons with workers in the same industry and in the same district, where employment circumstances were similar. But such comparisons with the going rate could be made only where no collective agreements existed. Schedule 11 also allowed claims to be pursued within the private sector only, but again on the basis of the comparison of wage rates being paid for similar work.

[2] Chris Pond, 'Back to the sweatshops?', *Low Pay Review*, November 1982.

[3] See David Jordan, 'Unfair Wages', *Low Pay Bulletin*, No. 30, December 1979.

On 28 July 1982 the Government announced its intention of rescinding the Fair Wages Resolution, putting forward five main arguments in favour of its abolition.[4] In the first place, it stressed that the Resolution was inconsistent with the Government's belief that pay and conditions should be determined by employers and unions according to the pressures of the market. Second, it argued that the Resolution was out of date. In his letter to interested parties on 25 May 1982 the Secretary of State commented:

over the years, social and economic conditions have changed considerably, as have relationships between employers and employees. Collective bargaining arrangements have increased to the extent where the great majority of employees have their pay and conditions of employment determined by agreed, voluntary arrangements in the light of the particular circumstances of the parties concerned. And the Government believes that provision for the imposition of other terms and conditions at the behest of one party can be disruptive of such arrangements and is in principle undesirable.

The Government's third reason centred on the belief that the Resolution was a barrier to employment, particularly in so far as it helped to price people out of jobs. Next, it was argued that an analysis of Fair Wages Resolution claims showed how the Resolution was not being used to help those in most need; the majority of claims came from relatively well-paid groups in highly unionised industries. The fifth line advanced by the Government, which to some extent countered many of its other arguments, was that the Resolution was now little used and was falling into abeyance. How do these claims stand up to examination, and particularly how true is it that 'the great majority of employees have their pay . . . determined by agreed voluntary arrangements'?

The latest information shows that 12,182,000 workers were in trade union membership in 1981, and this represents a fall of 5.9 per cent on the previous year. In that year too, 1980, union membership had also fallen by 3.7 per cent from a total of 13,447,000 members – the post-war peak in union membership. A similar decline, although less steep, is recorded if one examines the rate of union density, which is measured by dividing the potential union membership by the actual membership. Union density stood at 55.4 per cent in 1979, falling to 53.6 per cent a year later, and again to 51 per cent in 1981.[5]

The Employment Secretary might try to use these figures to support

[4] Summarised by Celia Nield, *Fair Wages Resolution*, House of Commons Research Note No. 99, 1982.

[5] Robert Price and George Sayers Bain, 'Union growth in Britain: retrospect and prospect', *British Journal of Industrial Relations*, March 1983, table 1.

his claim that 'the great majority of employees' have their pay and conditions determined by collective agreements. In his favour is the fact that many non-trade unionists work in establishments where pay is determined by the efforts of their trade union colleagues. But his assertion has less validity once we examine the level of unionisation in the private sector where the vast majority of government contracts are placed. Two areas which can be expected to gain a greater number of government contracts under current privatisation proposals are those classified as private services and the construction industry. Union membership in the former stands at less than 20 per cent, whereas in the construction industry it has fallen over recent years and by 1979 stood at 36.7 per cent.[6]

But not all union members have their pay set by collective agreements. While union membership stood at around 12 million in 1982, government estimates put only 10.7 million manual employees as being covered by national collective agreements and statutory wages orders.[7]

Other arguments were put to the Government against abolition. Incomes Data Services suggested, for example, that periods of more conventional incomes policy would return, despite current opposition, and that in such periods the Fair Wages Resolution 'acted as a priceless safety valve for particular pay pressures, especially in nationalised industries'.[8] IDS also questioned whether 'it is right in principle that those in a relatively favoured position of government contractor should not be contractually bound to act fairly to their employees'. This was a question left unanswered by the Government when it gained the approval of the House of Commons in December 1982 to abolish the Resolution.

Schedule 11

The protection given by Schedule 11 was abolished in 1980. The case the Government advanced was as follows: the main objective of Schedule 11 was held to be the abolition of 'pockets of low pay', but this had not been borne out in reality for 'many higher paid groups . . . benefited from awards'. In developing this line, the Government claimed that 'the majority of claims have been in respect of employees who could not be regarded as low paid on any absolute test'. But no-one argues in terms of an absolute definition of low pay; all the definitions

[6] George Sayers Bain and Robert Price, 'Union Growth: dimensions, determinants and density in George Sayers Bain (ed.), *Industrial Relations in Britain* (Basil Blackwell, 1983) Table 1.4.

[7] *House of Commons Hansard*, 25 July 1983, 322–3.

[8] Income Data Services, *Report* 379, June 1982.

considered at the PSI Conference, for example, were on a comparative basis. More to the point is an examination of what the wage levels were of those workers who benefitted from Schedule 11 claims.

Such an analysis has been undertaken by the Industrial Relations Research Unit at the University of Warwick, which examined the claims made under the Schedule 11 procedure for the period 1977-9. In 1977, the Unit's analysis of those claims which were successful showed that 97 were on behalf of manual workers earning less than median earnings, and only 21 came from manual workers earning above this level. The equivalent figures for non-manual workers were 96 and 4 respectively. In the following year, 1978, 95 of the successful claims under the Schedule were for manual workers earning less than median earnings, and only 5 for manual workers earnings above this average. Equivalent figures of non-manual workers were 82 and 18 respectively. The data for 1979 show an even greater number of successful claims being made on behalf of workers earning less than median earnings. Of the successful claims for manual workers, 93 per cent were on behalf of workers earning less than the average, and only 7 per cent for those earning above this level. For non-manual workers the picture was 87 and 13 per cent respectively.[9] Despite evidence of this kind which challenged the main reason put forward by the Government for abolition, the 1980 Employment Act abolished the Schedule 11 procedure.

Talking down wages

In the previous chapter an analysis was made of the extent of low pay in wages council industries as well as the proportion of all low-paid workers employed in this sector. While 25 per cent of all workers were found to be low-paid in 1982 (defined as earning less than two-thirds average earnings), a little over 70 per cent of all wages council employees were so categorised, despite the fact that the wages council sector employs less than 14 per cent of all employees. Yet it is this sector, employing a disproportionate number of low-paid, which has been singled out for a two-pronged government campaign aimed at reducing the level of wage settlements.

The first campaign has been public, and has been largely conducted in the House of Commons. Here Ministers have expressed unease at the level of wage settlements agreed by different wages councils, and particularly the rates paid to young workers. On one occasion, when the Employment Secretary was asked whether the level of settlements in

---

[9] Linda Dickens et al., 'A response to the Government working papers on amendments to employment protection legislation' (Industrial Relations Research Unit, University of Warwick, mimeograph, November 1979).

the wages council sector was preventing employers recruiting more workers, he replied:[10]

> It is self-evident that wages are ultimately limited by the ability of employers to pay, which is, in turn, limited by the prices which, in the light of home and overseas competition, they are able to obtain for their products. There is, therefore, little doubt that the higher the level at which councils set minimum wages the fewer people will be employed.

The questioner had asked the Employment Secretary if he would commission a survey to investigate the effect of wages council settlements on employment levels, and he had replied: 'I am doubtful that a survey could readily quantify this effect, i.e. the effect on the employment level.' Similarly, in an earlier debate, his junior Minister, after expressing the 'need to avoid high wage settlements for young people which can damage their employment prospects', was challenged to show that young workers' wage levels were pricing them out of jobs. The Minister could only reply that there was 'evidence from research studies supplied in confidence' to the Department.[11]

Running concurrently with Ministers expressing public concern about the level of wages council settlements has been a privately conducted correspondence with the chairman and members of individual wages councils, little of which has been made public. In fact, since 1979, the Government has written directly to wages councils on five separate occasions. The first was in July 1980 when an Employment Minister contacted the chairmen of the two retail wages councils; retail wages councils employ 37 per cent of all workers in the wages council sector. His purpose in writing was:

> to seek the views and the assistance of the Council on a matter which is frequently put to me in criticism of the operation of the wages council system. This concerns the position of the very small shopkeeper and the part time worker he employs. It has been represented to me that the council's awards are not designed with these people's needs sufficiently in mind and that the effect is to reduce opportunities for employment, especially for young people and for women.

In a letter dated 15 October 1980 to the members of all the wages councils the Government attempted to prevent them from making retrospective increases in statutory minimum rates. The Minister told the members that this was a question 'which has been raised with me frequently in recent months, especially by Members of Parliament on behalf of their constituents'. In another letter dated 27 August 1981,

---

[10] *House of Commons Hansard*, 6 July 1982, 139.

[11] *ibid.*, 4 March 1982, 223–4.

again to members of all the wages councils, the Government drew attention to its Young Workers Scheme. The purpose of the scheme was

> to encourage employers to recruit more young people at realistic wage rates. I am sure you will share the Government's concern about the level of youth unemployment, and our view that it is vital to get more young people into jobs. I hope that, as a member of a wages council, you will keep in mind the central purpose of the new scheme – a better chance for our young people – and take its provisions into account when coming to decision on the appropriate minimum rates to set for young people.

The fourth direct communication between the Government and those operating the wages council machinery occurred in February 1982 when an Employment Minister wrote on 24 February to all members of the two retail wages councils. The Minister began by observing that he expected 'to be approached from time to time by individuals and organisations concerned with the working of a wages council's system'. He went on to record how, in recent weeks, 'I have noted a change in both the nature and volume of the concern expressed to me. Much of this appears to have been promoted by the proposals which your councils have recently published.'

The effect these letters had on the decisions of what are supposed to be independent bodies is uncertain. Whatever it was, the Government was clearly unhappy with the results for, in a fifth letter dated 25 February 1983 to the two retail wages council chairmen, the Secretary of State commented on the proposed increase in minimum rates from April 1983:

> I have received many letters from small and large businesses alike about these proposals. It is abundantly clear that, if not modified, the proposals will have damaging effects on employment in the retailing industry. I trust you will give the most serious consideration to the representations on this point that you will no doubt receive.

The original recommendation was for an 8 per cent rise in the minimum rates. After representation from the Employment Secretary the councils reduced the increase to 6 per cent from April 1983 with the remaining two per cent delayed until October. The lowest minimum rate in retailing before the 1983 proposals came into effect stood at 93 pence an hour.

Conclusion

This chapter has examined the means and extent to which the position of the low-paid has deteriorated still further since 1979. While the tax burden has risen for practically all taxpayers, it has risen fastest for those on low pay, and particularly for those with children. The RPI rose by 54 per cent during the 1979/83 Parliament, but the index measuring the cost of living for low wage earners rose by almost a further 4 percentage points. The Government was successful in abolishing the Fair Wages Resolution and Schedule 11; both of these mechanisms were designed to protect and improve the pay of low wage earners. At the same time, there was a determined campaign by the Government 'to talk down' wage settlements. A specific campaign on the level of settlements in the wages councils was conducted both by the issuing of public ministerial statements, and by a sustained correspondence with the chairmen and members of certain wages councils. For a government that believes workers must price themselves into jobs, the publication of data showing increases in the number of low-paid will be viewed as a success. Before outlining ways of achieving more conventional successes for the low-paid, the discussion now turns to the importance of low pay as a major cause of poverty.

3 The Link with Poverty and Other Forms of Disadvantage

A number of delegates at the PSI conference – reflecting a strongly held view in this country – insisted that there was no link between low pay and poverty, and went on to argue that a national minimum wage was therefore a highly inefficient way of tackling that poverty which still exists. The present chapter disputes this view. It argues that low pay is a prime cause of poverty – both directly and indirectly – an argument which is central to the contention of this book.

Low pay and poverty

Seebohm Rowntree is a key contributor to our discussions. As we shall see later, Rowntree was the first person to attempt a 'scientific' definition of poverty, the results of which he set out in his pioneering study on the extent of poverty in York. This was published in 1901 and a follow-up study – carried out in 1936 – appeared during the Second World War[1]. These two surveys had a considerable impact on public opinion, confirming the impression of many observers and commentators that poverty was a major social problem, and that much, although not all, of it was caused directly by low pay. In contrast to the findings of these earlier studies, Rowntree's third and final study of poverty in York presented a radically different picture.[2] The advent of the welfare State, together with a steadily rising national income, had, according to Rowntree, almost eliminated pre-war poverty. His 1950 message was that what poverty remained was almost exclusively linked to old age. The findings from each of the Rowntree surveys on the importance of low pay as an immediate cause of poverty are presented in Table 3.1.

The publication in 1965 of *The Poor and the Poorest*[3] challenged Rowntree's assertion that poverty had been reduced to insignificant proportions, and that low pay was no longer its immediate cause. The

---

[1] B.S. Rowntree, *Poverty: A Study of Town Life* (Macmillan, 1901) and *Poverty and Progress* (Longman, 1941).

[2] B.S. Rowntree, *Poverty and the Welfare State* (Longman, 1951).

[3] Brian Abel-Smith and Peter Townsend, *The Poor and the Poorest* (Bell, 1965).

study, which was based on an analysis of the 1960 Family Expenditure Survey, calculated that 7.5 million people were living below the poverty line (defined as up to 140 per cent of the national assistance scale rates) and that, of this total, approximately 32 per cent were living in households primarily dependent on earnings. It should be noted, however, that the figures in the table before 1960 may not be comparable with those of the later date. While Rowntree's poverty line was an 'adjusted' absolute poverty line[4], the 1960 data were calculated on the explicit assumption of relative poverty. No calculations have been undertaken to see if Rowntree established an equivalent point in relation to average earnings, like the supplementary benefit definition.

Table 3.1 Low wages as an immediate cause of poverty

	No. in poverty due to low wages as a percentage of all individuals in poverty
1880	55
1936	37
1950	1
1960	32

Source: A.B. Atkinson, *Economics of Inequality* (OUP, 1975) p. 200.

Following the publication of *The Poor and the Poorest*, Abel-Smith and Townsend sought funds to undertake a nationwide poverty survey. The results were written up by Peter Townsend and published in 1979 under the title *Poverty in the United Kingdom*. This national survey showed that as many as 14 per cent of men, while experiencing no interruptions of employment for sickness or unemployment, were living in 1968 in, or on the margins of, poverty. They represented 1,450,000 working men out of a total of 10,400,000 whose earnings were not affected by absence from work. For a further 1,300,000 men, absence from work reduced their income to such an extent that they also were living in, or on the margins of, poverty. These figures, moreover, took no account of the number of low-paid women workers, or the importance of a second wage in raising a family's income above the poverty line. 'If married women's earnings were discounted, the proportion of families with men in full-time work who are in poverty or near-poverty would increase by over 50 per cent.'[5]

---

[4] See Frank Field, *Poverty and Politics*, op. cit., Chap. 8.

[5] Peter Townsend, *Poverty in the United Kingdom* (Penguin Books, 1979), pp. 629–31.

Later research on the importance of women's earnings in preventing family poverty suggests that this figure is an under-estimation. As the minority signatories to the report of the Royal Commission on the Distribution of Income and Wealth on *Lower Incomes* made clear:[6]

One reason that low pay . . . does not emerge as a more important cause of low family income is because families where the woman is earning are rarely amongst the lowest income families in a particular year.

In fact, one study carried out specially for the Royal Commission showed that there would be a trebling of the number of poor families if it were not for the incomes of working wives.[7]

Under-estimation of poverty

More recent evidence on the importance of low pay as a cause of poverty comes from the special analysis the Government regularly makes of the FES data. These results, first published in 1972, give information on the numbers of poor for each year through to 1979, except for 1978. In 1980 the Government announced that information for 1978 would not be published, and that in future the special analysis would be published only every other year. While the FES data are important, presenting as they do the most up-to-date information we have on the numbers of poor, there are five ways by which they under-estimate the extent of poverty in our society.

In the first place, a survey from which the estimates are taken is vulnerable to sampling error. The survey represents approximately a one-in-three-thousand sample. Estimates themselves are rounded to the nearest 10,000 to take account of this.

Second, the definition of income used for the analysis of the data also leads to an under-estimation of the numbers of poor. The FES is intended to yield information on expenditure patterns and experience has shown that these patterns do not vary greatly with short-term changes in income. Accordingly households in the sample are assessed according to their 'normal' income. This procedure results, for example, in those who have been unemployed for less than three months (in April 1983 these totalled 793,000) being treated as if they are still receiving the wage level earned prior to unemployment. This use of 'normal' income can make a considerable difference to the numbers of poor. Fiegehen, Lansley and Smith estimated that the proportion of individuals below the supplementary benefit level would have in-

---

[6] Cmnd 7175 (HMSO 1978) p. 156.

[7] R. Layard, D. Piachaud and M. Steward, *The Causes of Poverty* (HMSO, May 1978), p. 25.

creased by about a third if 'this week's income' were used instead of 'normal' income.[8]

Third, the FES survey presents estimates for those whose annual income is below the supplementary benefit level and this leads to an under-estimation of the numbers of poor *during* the year. There may be some families who are poor for part of the year, through spells of unemployment or sickness, but whose income for the rest of the year pulls their annual average income above the poverty level. These individuals and families do not appear in the FES estimates, which are a 'snap-shot' view of the numbers of poor at any one time.

The fourth reason why the FES data minimise the numbers on low incomes is the methodoligical change in analysing the data from 1979 onwards. This change concerns the way the data, which are collected at different times during the year, are standardised before being matched against the current benefit rates. The new method assesses all income in relation to the benefit rates in operation in December of each year. December is the first month following the annual up-rating and, as a result of this change, most people's income is compared with the benefit rates of up to a year previously.[9] How big a difference this change makes to the numbers of poor can be seen from the 1977 data where the Government has set out both sets of calculations. The results show that the method now employed in standardising income reduced the number of families in poverty in 1977 by 6.6 per cent and the number of individuals by 7.9 per cent, compared with the previous method.

Those people living in institutions are not covered by the FES enquiries, and their exclusion is the fifth means by which the data under-estimate the numbers on low income. Surveys of people in institutions, which range from doss-houses and hostels to old people's homes, show that many of the inmates live on very low levels of income indeed, and their inclusion in the survey would add to the numbers shown to be living at or below the supplementary benefit poverty level.

The results of the special analysis of the FES data are presented in Table 3.2.

Despite all the reservations about how these data are likely to under-estimate the extent of poverty, and particularly the numbers of low wage earners, the FES results nevertheless show just how significant low pay is as a cause of poverty. Even if we add in all the poor, including those over pensionable age, we see just how important low pay is as a

---

[8] G.C. Fiegehen, P.S. Lansley and A.D. Smith, *Poverty and Progress in Britain 1953-73* (CUP, 1977).

[9] See Liz Bissett, 'Poverty at Work', *Low Pay Review*, May 1983.

Table 3.2 FES(a) data on the numbers of poverty(b) wage earners

YEAR	Numbers in poverty due to low wages	
	as a percentage of all individuals in poverty	as a percentage of the poor below retirement age
1972	14	—
1973	16	—
1974	25	—
1975	26	42
1976	31	46
1977	27	41
1977 (c)	26	37
1979 (c)	17	30

(a) The data are not strictly comparable as the self-employed were omitted in 1972 and 1973.
(b) Defined as up to 140 per cent of the supplementary benefit entitled.
(c) Change in the figures from calculations based on income at the end of each year to an average over the whole year.
Source: DHSS: *Low Income Families*; various years.

cause. In recent years, while the numbers made poor by low pay have not fallen below 17 per cent, or around one in six of the total number of poor, they have risen as high as 31 per cent – almost one in three of all those in poverty. These results are presented in the middle column of Table 3.2.

But the real significance of low pay as a cause of poverty can be seen in the table's final column. This looks at the total of poor who are below retirement age, and calculates the importance of low pay as a cause of their poverty. The latest available figures, for 1979, show that 30 per cent, or almost one in three of the poor below retirement age, are poor owing to low wages. This is the lowest figure recorded in the column, and no doubt owes something to the then Labour Government's major injection of funds into the child benefit scheme from 1977 onwards. Prior to this move, in 1976, the numbers made poor by low wages stood at 46 per cent of the total number of poor below retirement age.

In two further respects, the official data in Table 3.2 under-estimate the importance of low pay as a cause of poverty. First, as stated above, the FES data present a 'snap-shot' view of the numbers of poor; they therefore give us only a total of those living in poverty at any one point in time. Yet the poor do not comprise a static army, and while some people remain poor for long periods of time, and possibly for the whole of their lives, others experience poverty for shorter time-spans. The extent to which some people may be subjected to low pay for part of their working life is illustrated in a special analysis of the NES for 1970, 1971 and 1972. This showed that while only 4.6 per cent of the sample were included in the lowest decile of earnings in all three years, a further 12.2 per cent were sometimes above the lowest tenth, and sometimes in it.[10] In other words, 16.8 per cent of all workers, or almost one in six, were low paid (defined as being in the lowest decile) during at least one of the three years in question.

Secondly, the official figures are an under-estimate because they do not recognise the extent to which low pay at any one time in a person's life can cause poverty in later years. We now turn to examine this issue.

Indirect cause of poverty: unemployment

Low pay is an indirect cause of poverty because, in Professor Atkinson's words, it is 'part of a more extended pattern of labour market disadvantage'.[11] This indirect effect can be seen in two ways: in the distribution of unemployment and in the pattern of sickness.

Nicholas Bosanquet was one of the first to present the unequal distribution of unemployment. Analysing the 1966 data, at a time when the average level of unemployment stood at 2.6 per cent, he found that the rate for professional workers and those in supervisory grades was 0.6 and 1.3 per cent respectively. At the other end of the social scale, the unemployment rate for personal service workers and unskilled manual workers was 4.9 and 6.8 per cent respectively.[12]

More recent information comes from the DHSS Cohort Study of unemployed men, which looked at unemployed men registering in 1978. The relevant information is presented in Table 3.3.

The table contains two pieces of information. First, it details the proportion in each socio-economic group as found in the Cohort Study of those unemployed who had been in full-time work in the year before registration. It also contains the SEG distribution of all economically active men as found in the General Household Survey. The comparison of these two sets of figures shows that, even though unemployment had increased 10.5-fold since Nicholas Bosanquet's study, its unequal distribution was still apparent. Whereas professional workers made up 7 per cent of economically active men, they accounted for only 2 per cent of the unemployed. At the other end of the social scale, semi-

---

[10] 'Low pay and changes in earnings', *Employment Gazette*, April 1973, p. 337.

[11] A.B. Atkinson, 'Low pay and the cycle of poverty' in Frank Field (ed.), *Low Pay* (Arrow, 1973), p. 102.

[12] N. Bosanquet, 'Government and unemployment, 1966–1970', *British Journal of Industrial Relations*, July 1974.

Table 3.3 Socio-economic groups, unemployed men 1978

	Unemployed (short study) %	Economically active men aged 20–69 (GHS) %
Professional	2	7
Employers and managers	8	16
Intermediate and junior non-manual	15	18
Skilled manual	38	41
Semi-skilled manual	24	15
Unskilled manual	13	4

Source: DHSS Cohort Study of the Unemployed, Working Paper No. 1, 1982, Table 32.

skilled manual workers, while amounting to 15 per cent of the employed population, constituted 24 per cent of the unemployed, and unskilled manual workers, who made up only 4 per cent of economically active men, contributed 13 per cent of the unemployed.

Sickness

There is ample evidence that low-paid workers are much more likely to experience sickness than other groups of workers, although it is uncertain whether this is due to 'a general link between low living standards and sickness' or if there is a 'specific correlation between low-paid jobs and occupation-related diseases'.[13] The most recent information from the General Household Survey illustrates the following pattern of sickness. Respondents were asked if they suffered from any long-standing illness and their replies were analysed by age, sex and socio-economic group. For men the percentage of respondents reporting a long-standing illness rose from 16 per cent of professional workers aged between 16 and 44 to 29 per cent for unskilled manual workers. The respective figures for the 45–64 age group were about 35 per cent and 43 per cent. The relationship was not quite as clear for women workers, although the percentage reporting illness amongst semi-skilled and unskilled manual workers was higher than all other groups, and this was true for both age groups.[14]

The Black Report, published in 1980, commented that the 'persistence of class differentials in both mortality and morbidity is

---

[13] Atkinson, 'Low pay and the cycle of poverty', *op. cit.*, p. 111.

[14] *General Household Survey 1980* (HMSO 1982), table 7.4.

evidenced in regular reports provided by the OPCS'.[15] It also remarked (pp. 29–30) that, while the GHS poses questions on health, 'detailed analyses of trends on an annual basis are difficult because of the restricted size of the sample and there is no opportunity to examine a longer time series'.

Following the publication of this report, the DHSS carried out a special analysis of the 1976 GHS to investigate the link between health and a range of socio-economic variables, including income. The results confirmed that when income is considered in isolation there is 'some evidence that the proportion of males and females reporting *no long-standing illness rises with income*' and 'the degree to which the persistence of long-standing illness restricts activities shows evidence of falling as income rises'.[16]

While low-paid workers experience higher sickness rates than other groups of workers, they are less likely to be covered by occupational sick pay schemes. Companies have a statutory duty to provide sick pay for the first eight weeks of sickness in any tax year, with the rates of benefit laid down by the Government. It is only at the ninth week of sickness that employees become eligible to be paid sickness benefit directly from the State scheme.

Running alongside the State scheme are company sick pay schemes and many of these discriminate in favour of higher-paid workers in the following ways. First, there is a difference in coverage. The 1977 DHSS report showed 94.2 per cent of those in non-manual occupations being covered by sick pay schemes, compared with only 74 per cent of those in manual occupations. The equivalent figures for married women were 92.8 and 57.9 per cent respectively.[17] Coverage also varies according to the industry in which a worker is employed. While almost all men employed in public administration, gas, electricity, water and mining have a right to occupational sick pay, only 50 per cent of male leather workers and 51 per cent of male textile workers come within a company sick pay scheme.

Secondly, sick pay schemes discriminate against lower paid workers through the qualifying periods for benefit. According to IDS, a minimum period of service in order to qualify for occupational sick pay 'is fairly common – particularly for manual workers'.[18] The 1977 DHSS

[15] *Report of the Working Party on Inequalities in Health* (DHSS, 1980), p. 29.

[16] Andrew Burchell, *Inequalities in Health: Analysis of the 1976 GHS*, (GES Working Paper 48, 1981).

[17] DHSS, *Report on a Survey of Occupational Sick Pay Schemes* (HMSO, 1977).

[18] IDS, Study 283, 1983, p. 4.

study found that 48 per cent of full-time female employees and 68 per cent of full-time male employees were required to serve a qualification period. And it is important here to remember the extent to which low-paid workers are more likely than other workers to change employment – and thus to lose rights to sickness benefit – in order to stave off unemployment.

The third means by which discrimination occurs stems from the structure of the schemes. First there are those schemes based on the flat-rate principle where each employee receives a set amount of money for each day's or week's sickness. Generally speaking, these schemes make the same payment to all members of the scheme, regardless of the status or the average weekly pay of the employee. Then there are what are called percentage schemes which guarantee a specific level of sick pay, either at the full pay level of 100 per cent or as a proportion of an employee's full pay. Flat-rate schemes are more egalitarian than percentage schemes in that a set level of sick pay will form a higher proportion of the normal pay of a low-paid worker than for other company employees. But flat-rate schemes are far rarer than percentage schemes; the 1977 DHSS report found only 13 per cent of men and 6 per cent of women were covered by flat-rate schemes.

The failure to gain similar occupational sick pay coverage, and on equal terms, to other groups of the working population results in lower-paid workers being reduced to a very low standard of living during sickness. And as low-paid workers have fewer other financial resources on which to fall back during this time, they are therefore much more likely to be made poor as a result of their greater propensity to sickness.

Old age
The most obvious way by which poverty caused by low pay can lead to poverty later in life relates to poverty in old age. Those who have been fortunate enough to earn a high income are likely to be in a position to buy their own house and possibly acquire an occupational pension. Such people are very unlikely to find themselves living on a very low income in old age. A low-paid worker, on the other hand, will have had little chance to acquire his own house, is less likely to have acquired an occupational pension, and is still more unlikely to have managed to build up any substantial savings. Professor A.B. Atkinson has commented on how low earnings can be a cause of poverty in old age:[19]

There are many forces making for the continuity of poverty and its reoccurrence with predictable frequency ... low pay is a thread which runs

---

[19] Atkinson, 'Low pay and the cycle of poverty', *op. cit.*

throughout people's working life-times, and goes beyond into retirement and what may appear at first sight to be 'bad-luck' is likely to be related to labour market disadvantage. Poverty does not happen to just anyone.

The extent to which low pay locks a person into poverty in old age can be seen by piecing together information on the State and occupational pension schemes. In the State scheme every employee pays contributions towards what is now called the basic pension. Contributions are also made for an additional pension for all those employees not contracted out of the State scheme, and much stress has been put on the fact that the additional pension was designed to favour low earners.

The scheme started in 1978 and in all the official projections the value of future pensions was compared with current earning levels. A worker on £40.00 a week, for example, would, if single, gain a pension after 20 years' contributions of 58 per cent of previous earnings and, if married, 84 per cent. A worker on £80.00 a week (average earnings in 1978 were £89.10 a week) would gain a pension after 20 years' contributions of 36 per cent of previous income if single, and 45 per cent if married.

There have been no firm calculations of whether the new pension scheme will break the link between poverty and old age. All the suggestions have been that it will succeed in doing so, but the following calculations cast doubt on this. Working on 1978 data, we find that the vast majority of pensioners claiming supplementary pensions were single (1.3 out of 1.6 million claimants). On average, these claimants drew £7.40 a week in addition to their £19.50 old-age pension, to make their total income £26.90 a week. But the projection pension in 1978 prices for a pensioner who had previously earned £40.00 a week was, after 20 years' contributions, £23.15: in other words, a pension less than he would gain under the existing pension scheme plus help from the supplementary benefit scheme. Indeed, it is not until one approaches average earnings that the new pension scheme will be paying out benefit generous enough to raise people above the supplementary benefit poverty line.

Those who have contracted out of having their additional pension provided by the State will be members of occupational pension schemes. At regular intervals the Government Actuary publishes reports on occupational pension schemes. One such report was published in 1971 and it is cited here because it is the most recent report to give a break-down of manual, and non-manual membership. It shows a fall in the number of workers covered by occupational pensions; down from 62 to 58 per cent. This fall disguised a widening gap between manual and non-manual workers. Whereas the number of male non-manual workers increased from 85 to 87 per cent, the number of male manual workers covered by an occupational pensions scheme had fallen from 64 to 56 per cent. Similarly, the number of non-manual female workers covered rose from 53 to 56 per cent, while the number of manual female workers fell from 21 to 18 per cent.

The report also examined the bases on which occupational pensions were calculated. Broadly, there are three such calculations. The first bases a worker's pension on the earnings he drew during the closing years or months of his employment. The second links the pension payments to the salary earned throughout the worker's career. The third pays a flat amount independent of previous earnings. The first method is most favourable to higher paid workers, and 85 per cent of professional workers were covered by this kind of scheme. The least favourable calculation is the third; 59 per cent of all manual workers in a pension scheme were covered by this means of calculation.

The most recent Government Actuary's Report is for 1979 and this shows an increase in the number of workers covered by occupational schemes. But while there has been a rise from 11.4 million members in 1975 to 11.8 million in 1979, the increase disguises a fall in the number of male workers in the private sector who are paying towards an occupational pension. Likewise, the 1979 report shows just how extensive is the number of workers in the private sector who are not covered; 4.8 million not in a pension scheme compared to 4.7 million who are. The figures for women workers are even more extreme; only 1.5 million out of a total of 6.2 million are earning occupational pension rights.[20]

Three pieces of information in this latest report point to a continuing discrimination against lower-paid workers. Evidence shows that, on the whole, the smaller the firm the lower is the pay. More employees in smaller firms than in larger firms have no occupational pension rights[21]. Similarly, part-time workers are generally lower paid than other workers. Only 150,000 part-time women workers, out of an estimated 2.4 million, are within an occupational pension scheme[22]. In addition, the most commonly used pension formula to calculate entitlement discriminates against many low-paid workers. Since 1971 there has been an increase in the number of schemes using a final salary formula as the basis for pension calculations; by 1979 90 per cent of cases do just this[23]. Manual workers' earnings usually fall in relative terms as they

---

[20] Government Actuary, *Occupational Pension Schemes 1979*, (HMSO, 1981), table 2.8.

[21] *ibid.*, table 5.3.

[22] *ibid.*, table 2.9.

[23] *ibid.*, p. 40.

approach retirement. Not so with higher paid workers who often receive special salary boosts – in order to increase their pension rights – in their final working years.

Conclusion

The evidence presented here from the FES shows that during the 1974–9 period low pay was a direct cause of poverty for between 30 and 40 per cent of those below pensionable age who were found to be poor. These figures alone begin to undermine the case of those who argue that low pay is no longer one of poverty's recruiting sergeants. When we add in the extent to which low pay is an indirect cause of poverty amongst those who are unable to continue working, and is inextricably bound up with other forms of disadvantage, the conventional argument on the unimportance of low pay as the cause of poverty begins to look very shaky indeed. Yet, somewhat ironically, many of those who minimise the role of low pay as a cause of poverty still assert the importance of the 'incentive to work' problem or, as it is sometimes called, 'the why-work syndrome'.[24] We now turn to look at this aspect of the current debate.

---

[24] Ralph Howell, the Norfolk MP who coined the phrase 'why-work syndrome', is an honourable exception; practically all Howell's public statements have emphasised the extent of low pay and the importance of introducing a minimum wage.

4 The Poverty Trap and Incentives to Work

The theme of this chapter is almost that of a parable. It examines how the failure both to tackle directly the issue of low pay, and to build up a generous system of child support paid to all families, including those in work, has led Tory and Labour Governments alike to introduce a range of means-tested supplements. It shows that the problems thereby created, while different, have been almost as serious as those the measures were intended to eradicate; and that the opting for what appeared to be the cheapest policy resulted in large unforeseen costs.

At the present time there are over forty means-tested benefits, although not all of these concern the poor in work. Those which are central to the argument here are the family income supplement (FIS), free school meals and rent and rate rebates. The chapter looks first at the rise of the means-test welfare State before going on to explain the 'poverty trap'. This is followed by a section on the 'incentives to work' and the 'why-work syndrome', and the concluding section reviews the Social Democratic Party's proposals for dealing with these issues.

Means-tested welfare

Towards the end of 1942 the Beveridge proposals, with their aim of abolishing poverty by 'ensuring that every citizen . . . has at all times an income to meet his responsibilities' [1] were greeted with a blaze of publicity. While part of this fanfare was no doubt due to Lord Longford's flair with the media (as Frank Pakenham, he was at this time Beveridge's research assistant), it was also very much in response to what the newspapers judged to be the electorate's wish to put behind them the poverty of the 1930s. The reasons why these proposals did not achieve their objective have been recalled elsewhere.[2] What concerns us here is the result of the whittling down of the original Beveridge objectives – or rather, what the electorate saw as these objectives, for there were flaws in the proposals from the very beginning. They failed to provide an income as of right, free of means tests, and generous

---

[1] *Social Insurance and Allied Services*, Cmd 6404, (HMSO 1942) p. 165.

[2] See Frank Field, *Inequality in Britain: Freedom, Welfare and the State* (Fontana, 1981), chap. 4.

enough to take a recipient's income above whatever the State defined as a poverty line. This resulted in large numbers having to claim means-tested assistance and, as many people refused the help on this basis, in increasing numbers living on a very low income indeed. Moreover, and of more importance to the theme of this book, Beveridge assumed that the wage system was adequate to cover the needs of a husband and wife together with one child. His benefit for families in work – family allowances – was therefore paid only to second and subsequent children and, like his other proposals, this too was scaled down in value. But Beveridge's assumption about the value of wages was wrong when he made it[3] and was seen to be so by the 1960s. Two important repercussions have followed from these miscalculations.

First, there has been a steady increase in the number of working poor claiming means-tested assistance. Second, governments have shied away from providing universal assistance in the form of family allowances or child benefits, and have relied instead on extending the range of means-tested help. Means-tested benefits, together with the falling tax threshold, have resulted in what has become known as the 'poverty trap'.

The three means-tested benefits which make up the poverty trap are: free school meals, rent and rate rebates, and FIS. The calculations for the Beveridge Report assumed that school dinners would be provided free. When parents were charged, exceptions were made for families on low income, but free school meals alone, or combined with rate and rent rebates (introduced in 1967 and 1972 respectively), would not have resulted in high marginal rates of tax for low-income families. The decisive factor was the introduction of FIS in 1971.

Family income supplement

To trace the origins of FIS we need to return to the events of the mid-1960s[4]. A reference has already been made to the publication of *The Poor and the Poorest* in 1965, but not to the establishment some months earlier of the Child Poverty Action Group. Following Eleanor Rathbone, the main thrust of CPAG's campaign was to push for a significant increase in family allowances, since remodelled and renamed 'child benefits'. In 1970 the Group published a review of the then Labour Government's record as regards low-income families, and these findings were interpreted as 'the poor become poorer under Labour'. The campaign document aimed at winning an increase in

---

[3] *ibid.*, pp. 70 and 83.

[4] For a full introduction to FIS see Joan C. Brown, *Family Income Supplement* (PSI, 1983).

family allowances in the 1970 budget. It failed in this primary objective, but gained a commitment from the then Conservative Opposition leader, Edward Heath, and his Shadow Chancellor, Iain Macleod, that a future Tory government would increase family allowances on the grounds that this was the best method of tackling family poverty.[5]

In order to limit the cost of paying a universal increase in family allowances to mothers for all eligible children, CPAG had proposed that the increase should be clawed back by adjusting the child tax allowances; these allowances were invariably claimed by fathers. But as we have noted in Chapters 1 and 2, the tax threshold has been falling for decades, and civil servants were quick to point out to the Heath Government, once in office, the weakness in CPAG's proposal: the tax threshold was so low that practically all parents, including many of the poor, would have had the increase in family allowances clawed back through the tax system. Instead of raising the tax threshold, the Government cut the rates of tax and introduced a new benefit for low-income families in work called the Family Income Supplement. This benefit operated on the principle of setting an eligibility limit for help. Working families with children could claim help if their income was below this eligibility level, and payment was made at the rate of half the difference between a family's gross income and their FIS qualifying income level; for each £1.00 increase in a claimant's income, 50 pence was lost from FIS when the family renewed its claim. As the FIS eligibility level, which varied according to the size of the family, was set above the tax threshold, and because FIS families would also be eligible for other forms of means-tested help (particularly free school meals and what were then termed rent and rate rebates), the basis had been constructed for what became known later as the 'poverty trap'.[6]

Poverty trap

'Hundreds of thousands of trade unionists are not getting what they bargained for' is how the original article on the poverty trap began. It continued:

It is now a fact that for millions of low-paid workers very substantial pay increases have the absurd effect of increasing only marginally their family's net income and in some cases actually make the family worse off.

The effect on take-home pay of the overlap of the eligibility income levels for means-tested assistance and the tax and national insurance

---

[5] For fuller details of this side of the campaign, see Frank Field, *Poverty and Politics*, *op. cit.*, pp. 38–40.

[6] See Frank Field and David Piachaud, 'The Poverty Trap', *New Statesman*, 3 December 1981.

thresholds is illustrated in Table 4.1. The figures in the table relate to the tax year 1981/2 and are to be found in the SDP's green paper published in 1982, *Attacking Poverty*. They are used because they illustrate the salient features of the poverty trap debate, and will allow later a direct comparison with the effects on income of the SDP's own proposals to deal with the poverty trap.

Table 4.1 Net income of a couple with two children (£)

Weekly pay	(Rent £15, rates £5, all income earned by husband)				
	50	80	100	120	200
Current stystem					
Family Income Supplement	16.00	1.00	—	—	—
Free school meals	5.06	5.00	—	—	—
Rent rebate	12.76	9.01	5.80	2.40	—
Rate rebate	4.20	3.00	1.90	0.70	—
Child Benefit	10.50	10.50	10.50	10.50	10.50
−Tax	−2.62	−11.62	−17.70	−23.60	−47.60
−National Insurance	−3.87	−6.20	−7.70	−9.30	−15.50
Net Income	91.97	90.69	92.80	100.70	147.40

Source: SDP, *Attacking Poverty*, 1982, p. 6.

Table 4.1 shows just how little the income of a family with two children changes over the income bands from £50.00 to £120.00. Indeed, a family earning £50.00 a week gains only £8.73 net from a £70.00 increase in gross income.

The political response to the poverty trap debate has varied, usually according to whether the party spokesman was on the opposition or government benches. Opposition spokesmen have tended to emphasise the seriousness of this state of affairs; ministers have tended to stress that the poverty trap is a theoretical argument which does not tally with the day-to-day experiences of many of the poor.

The number of families facing high marginal rates of tax has been published in various editions of *Social Trends*; these figures show the number of families theoretically subject to a marginal tax rate of 100 per cent or more rising from 20,000 in 1974 to 50,000 in 1977. The 1979 figures report a falling to about 30,000 families with children who receive no increase in net income from an additional £1.00 in earnings.[7]

A more serious picture was presented in evidence to the House of

[7] *Social Trends 13* (HMSO, 1982), p. 74.

Commons Treasury and Civil Service Committee enquiring into the structure of personal income taxation and income support. Working from 1980 FES data, and assuming 100 per cent take-up of benefits, Professor A.B. Atkinson and his colleagues calculated the tax ratios on £1.00 of additional earnings. This analysis found that 700,000 households faced marginal tax rates of 50 per cent or more, and of these 40,000 faced 100 per cent or more marginal tax rates. The relevant data are reproduced in Table 4.2.

Table 4.2 Tax ratios on £1.00 additional earnings by head of tax units – 1980

Tax ratio (tax paid + benefits lost)	Estimated number of tax units in whole population*
50–59	190,000
60 (Income tax + NI contribution + rent and rate rebates)	310,000
61–69	40,000
70–79	60,000
80–89	20,000
90–99	40,000
100–	40,000

Note: *Rounded to the nearest 10,000. For this reason, the figures do not add exactly to the total. The estimates cover those tax units where the head, whether man or woman, is in full-time paid employment. They therefore exclude the heads of tax units who are self-employed, part-time workers or pensioners as well as those without work.
Source: Reproduced from Treasury and Civil Service Committee, *The Structure of Personal Income Taxation and Income Support*, Appendices, House of Commons Paper 20–II, HMSO, 1983, Table A.1.

That the position of low-paid workers is worsening in respect of the poverty trap is supported by two other sources of information. The Low Pay Unit, in its evidence to the Committee, presented the number of FIS recipients paying tax, and showed how this had changed over the years 1974 to 1981: FIS together with tax and national insurance contributions mount up to a 89 per cent marginal tax rate. In 1974, of the 75,210 FIS recipients, only 15,000, or 20 per cent, were estimated to be above the tax threshold when FIS was claimed in the previous year. By December 1981, 105,600, or 80 per cent of the 132,000 FIS beneficiaries, were above the tax threshold.[8]

The second piece of information comes from the Government itself. Its evidence to the Committee showed that a married couple with two

[8] Treasury and Civil Service Committee, *The Structure of Personal Income Taxation and Income Support*, Minutes of Evidence, House of Commons Paper 20–1, HMSO December 1982, Table 11, p. 15.

children in April 1982 could face a theoretical tax rate of more than 100 per cent over the income range from £47.00 to £82.00 per week; over these income bands 'a near doubling of gross earnings could mean a reduction in net income'.[9] And, as the Committee went on to observe, 'It appears that the range of gross incomes affected has been widening in recent years'.

The Treasury and Civil Service Committee ended its deliberations on the poverty trap by recording (p. xxiii of its Report):

> It is clear from the foregoing that the extreme version of the poverty trap so-called i.e. the problem of poor working families facing a marginal rate of 100 per cent, is only the tip of the iceberg.

It is a tip of the iceberg in another sense too. This complex of wage levels and tax rates which we have been examining also forms the basis for the 'unemployment trap', a topic to which we now turn.

Why-work syndrome

Ralph Howell was the first politician consistently to draw attention to the narrowness of the gap between the income of many low wage earners when in work and their benefit entitlement when they were without a job. Howell put his argument in the following terms.

The British economy is characterised not only by low wages but by income tax collected on levels of income below the State poverty line. The result is that the net income from work for many families affords them a standard of living which is at best very little above what they would experience if they were to stay at home. Indeed, a low-paid worker who works full-time may in some instances be worse off than if unemployed. This is not because the benefits payable to the unemployed are large; in fact, they are officially regarded as the minimum on which a family can manage to live.

In a pamphlet published at the beginning of 1976, Howell looked at the income of families on low wages, comparing their take-home pay when they were in work with the level of benefits to which they were entitled if they were unemployed. At that time, average weekly earnings stood at £71.80, and earnings-related supplement was still being paid. Howell reported:[10]

> The hardship imposed by long-term unemployment is considerable. Families will lose their right to an earnings related benefit and to FIS. There are, however, families who are unable to raise their standards of living very much

---

[9] Treasury and Civil Service Committee, *The Structure of Personal Income Taxation and Income Support*, House of Commons Paper 386, May 1983, p. xx.

[10] Ralph Howell, *Low Pay and Taxation*, Low Pay Paper No. 8, 1976.

above this meagre level, even if the bread winner works a full week, because of the need to pay tax, national insurance and work expenses. A job in which the husband works a full week and earns £20 will leave himself and his wife worse off than if he were receiving flat-rate unemployment benefit (plus housing rebates) or relying on supplementary benefit.

Even earning £25 a week, the couple will be left with only £18-25p more than they would receive on SB. A similar picture emerges if we consider the case of a two-child family whose bread winner normally earns low wages. With normal earnings of £35 a week, this family would pay £3.47 tax and £1.93 in national insurance contributions, leaving them (even after adding on FIS and family allowance) with £25.73 – just 73p more than if they relied on flat-rate unemployment benefit. A family of four can only secure a net income which is more than £2 a week higher than the family could expect on SB or with long-term unemployment benefit, if he works in a job which pays more than £45 a week.

Ever since Howell raised the spectre of the unemployment trap, the debate has raged on whether this too is merely part of the beholder's theoretical imagination. While there are exceptions, protagonists in the poverty trap debate swap sides on the issue; those who emphasise the importance of the poverty trap for the poor in work tend to minimise the effect of the unemployment trap, and vice versa.

The ratio of net income when unemployed to net income in work is measured by what is called the 'replacement rate'. Since 1979 the Government has taken three measures to lessen the replacement rate, i.e. to increase the gap between a person's income when in work compared with when he is drawing the dole. The earnings-related supplement, paid to eligible claimants during the first six months of unemployment, has been abolished; unemployment pay is now taxable; and tax rebates are not now paid immediately to those losing their jobs. How these measures have affected the replacement rates can be seen from Table 4.3.

Other factors also have an effect on the level of the replacement rate, for example, wage increases and the movement of rents and rates, together with benefit levels. As we can see from Table 4.3, over the period November 1978 to November 1982, short-term replacement rates have fallen; so too have long-term rates, but not by as much.

This has led a number of commentators to argue that the unemployment trap is now of little importance to the real world. Using the data in the table, an argument is advanced that, whereas 35 per cent or so of working families had a short-term replacement rate above 80 per cent in 1978, this had fallen to about 10 per cent by 1982. The main reason why radicals initially underplayed this issue would seem to be the fear that any other approach would add support to the campaign to cut unemployment benefit. While this was an honourable enough reason, it

Table 4.3 Distribution of replacement rates for the working population

Working Households with Replacement Rates Below	Percentages of all working households					
	November 1978		November 1980		November 1982	
	Short-Term	Long-Term	Short-Term	Long-Term	Short-Term	Long-Term
£						
40	2	10	3	25	14	23
50	7	31	10	47	36	45
60	21	56	28	67	59	65
70	43	75	51	84	78	83
80	65	88	72	93	90	93
90	82	94	86	96	96	97
100	92	97	95	98	98	99
110	97	98	98	99	99	99
Average Rate	74	60	71	53	58	54

Notes
1. Short-term means four weeks unemployment; long-term 52 weeks or more.
2. These calculations reflect the maximum that replacement rates can reach, as they relate to the position just after a benefit uprating. Prior to the November uprating in 1982, for example, the average long-term rate will be 52 per cent.

Source: Reproduced from IFS evidence to the Treasury and Civil Service Committee, *The Structure of Personal Income Taxation and Income Support*, Appendices, House of Commons Paper 20–II (HMSO, 1983), Table 3, p. 35.

was ineffective in preventing the cuts taking place. Moreover, it was a misplaced strategy, for, above all, it misunderstands how many working people respond to the choices they sometimes have over accepting or refusing jobs.

Admittedly, with present levels of unemployment, and with the numbers of long-term unemployed rapidly increasing, many claimants have no choice at all but to remain unemployed. But this is not true of all claimants. High unemployment does not mean that there are no jobs available. While the unemployment figures are always presented in terms of a total, it is more accurate to view them as a flow; each month some claimants join while others leave the roll. If more join than leave, the unemployment total increases, while the reverse is true if there are more ceasing to register themselves as unemployed than those signing on for the first time. In May 1983 over 452,000 people ceased to draw benefit, many (but not all) because they had obtained a job. So some claimants have the choice of taking jobs even at the current time of massively high unemployment.

The present author's experience of working with low-income groups for over 15 years has taught him that careful calculations are undertaken by some claimants as to how much better off they will be if a particular job is accepted. And some informants insist that their replacement rate – to use a phrase never encountered on the door-step or in a constituency advice surgery – has to be significantly below the 80 per cent rate to make it worthwhile to go out to work in what is often a boring, repetitive and sometimes a dirty and dangerous job.

This argument is not presented as ammunition for those who wish to cut the dole still further – although they may well use it. The case for increasing dole payments is overwhelming, but *no* government is going to do so while we have the problems of low wages and low child benefits. Only by presenting the issues honestly is there any hope of mobilising widespread support in the country for the necessary reforms. The Left has damaged its standing with all too many of its supporters by talking about a world its potential voters cannot recognise. The incentive to work debate is one such example. A full recognition of the extent of the disincentive to work which many people face strengthens the case for the minimum wage and child benefit strategy presented in this book. It also provides an appropriate backcloth to a discussion of the proposals put forward by the SDP for the poverty trap and the incentive to work questions.

SDP proposals

The introduction to this book commented on the growing support in centre-left radical circles for a national minimum wage. Only the SDP stands aloof, arguing that the low-wage problem – to the extent that it causes poverty – should be dealt with through the tax and benefit system. How workable are the alternative reforms put forward by the SDP?

In its policy statement *Attacking Poverty* the SDP remarked not only on the growing numbers of poor, but on the many who have 'no incentive to try and better their lot' (p. 1). To deal with this situation the party put forward two proposals.

It is known that not all families claim the means-tested help to which they are entitled. Recent government estimates suggest that up to 37 per cent of the sick and disabled and 20 per cent of the unemployed do not claim free school meals for their children, and possibly half of eligible families fail to claim FIS. The numbers affected by the poverty trap are lessened in direct proportion to the extent to which families do not claim means-tested help, but only at the 'cost' of these families being in worse poverty than they would otherwise be. The SDP's 'final aim is to eliminate claiming by making the payment of tax benefits (sic) automatic for those families that are entitled to them' (p. 2). But the words 'final aim' need to be stressed. The SDP admits than this can only be achieved after there has been a full computerisation of the tax system, and this is still some way off. In the meantime an 'interim scheme' is proposed.

The nature of this interim scheme is a proposal for a single Basic Benefit for working households which will take the place of FIS, rent and rate rebates and free school meals. (Since this proposal was written, the Government has remodelled the rent rebate scheme into a new housing benefit.) Unlike the present system, where a number of claims have to be made in order to ensure maximum help (although FIS does act as a passport to a range of other means-tested benefits), the SDP's system entails only a single application for the Basic Benefit. The effect of claiming this benefit on the income of low wage earners can be seen from Table 4.4.

Table 4.4 Net income of a couple with two children under Basic Benefit (£)

(Rent £15, rates £5, all income earned by husband)

	50	80	100	120	200
New System					
Basic Benefit Credit	75.00	75.00	75.00	75.00	} 0
−Withdrawal	−22.50	−36.00	−45.00	−54.00	
Child Benefit	10.50	10.50	10.50	10.50	10.50
−Tax	−7.30	−16.74	−23.04	−29.34	−54.54
−National Insurance	−3.87	−6.20	−7.75	−9.30	−15.50
Net Income	101.83	106.56	109.71	112.85	145.46
Change in Income	+9.86	+15.87	+16.94	+12.24	−1.91

Source: Reproduced from SDP, *Attacking Poverty*, 1982, table 2.

The income of the working poor would certainly increase. Comparing the figures in tables 4.1 and 4.4, we see that a two-child family earning £50.00 – who, under the present system, have their income raised to £91.97 a week providing they claim all the help to which they are entitled – gain an additional £9.86 weekly with Basic Benefit, bringing their income up to £101.83. A similar increase occurs to the income of other groups; a two-child family on £120.00 a week, whose income under the present tax and benefit system is reduced to £100.70, is increased to £112.85 a week – up by £12.24. But now let us look again at the poverty trap. Using table 4.1, we saw earlier that an increase of £70.00 on an original weekly wage of £50.00 left the family only £8.73 better off. Under the SDP's proposal, the same family, after earning an additional £70.00 a week, is still only £11.02 better off. Few low-income families will look on this as the abolition of the poverty trap. Indeed, the SDP plan would result in an increase in the range of incomes over which the poverty trap is effective.

The reason why the SDP's plan makes so little impact on the disincentive effect of the tax and benefit system is as follows. All means-tested benefits have to be withdrawn as income rises and, as the SDP rightly notes, 'in choosing the exact withdrawal rate there is a dilemma' (p. 7). A low rate of withdrawal results in help being spread way up the income scale; in the SDP's example, to almost twice average earnings. 'And we should not and cannot afford to subsidise people earning over £14,000 a year' (pp. 7–8). On the other hand, if help is concentrated on low-income groups – the aim of the proposal – then a high rate of withdrawal is required, but this again begins to build a poverty trap effect. This effect remains, even though the SDP opts for a 'middle position'; for families with children a withdrawal rate of 45 per cent is proposed. This rate, together with current tax and national insurance rates, gives a marginal tax rate of 84 per cent.

Means-tested benefits – such as FIS and rent and rate rebates – have a habit of taking on a permanent form. The SDP insists that its Basic Benefit is only an interim proposal. But computerisation of the tax and benefit system is still a long way off, and the experience of running the new Housing Benefit Scheme is none too reassuring even when computers are supposed to be helping to simplify the scheme. The SDP needs to look again at its interim proposals. They do not present a workable alternative to the proposals which will be discussed in the following section.

Conclusion

Low pay, together with a low tax threshold linked to high marginal rates of tax, underlies both the poverty trap and the unemployment trap. Both these situations have struck, and continue to strike, many voters as being unfair; there is a widely held view that if people work overtime or get a better-paid job they should be allowed to keep a substantial part of their increased earnings; many voters also believe that it is undesirable for people to find themselves little, if at all, better off when moving from unemployment back into the labour force. Both issues, the poverty trap and, to a lesser extent, the unemployment trap, have been used by campaigners to highlight the issue of low pay. This aspect of the campaign, together with a growing realisation about the numbers of low wage earners, the decline in the relative earnings of the low-paid, the effects of taxation and the differential impact of inflation, have all played a part in moving the low pay issue higher up the political agenda. A comprehensive programme to deal with these issues is outlined in the following chapters.

II
A COMPREHENSIVE POLICY AGAINST LOW PAY

The review in the previous section illustrates how the living standards of the low-paid are determined by a whole range of forces, and any effective policy to improve the relative position of the lowest-paid needs to take each of them into account. This section outlines the range of initiatives required to build a comprehensive policy to combat low pay and the low living standards of many low-paid workers. It begins by stressing the crucial role which the child benefit scheme has in any such programme, as well as its importance in discussions on a national minimum wage strategy. After looking at the level at which a NMW needs to be set, the discussion turns in Chapter 6 to look at the costs and benefits of a NMW. This is followed in Chapter 7 by a review of those compensatory measures which need to be taken in order to minimise the impact a NMW may have on employment and inflation. Chapter 8 is concerned with the basis for a trade union alternative to a NMW. The section continues by outlining the means by which the tax threshold can be raised, while at the same time cutting the rates of tax for those on low incomes. The final chapter is concerned with reforms of the Equal Pay and Sex Discrimination Acts.

5 Child Benefit and the National Minimum Wage

While discussions about the role of child benefit are important in their own right (and are summarised in Appendix 2) they also have a crucial relevance to the national minimum wage debate. As we saw in Chapter 3, low pay is still an important cause of poverty, and particularly family poverty. Yet, rather surprisingly, most of the public debate about the level at which the NMW needs to be set is put in terms of its relation to average earnings, rather than in relation to the poverty line. It is assumed in this debate that such a target minimum wage will be set at a high enough level automatically to abolish poverty. This chapter therefore begins by reviewing the level at which current demands for a minimum wage are put, before turning to examine how effective such a minimum wage would be in breaking the link between earnings and poverty.

The value of the NMW
To begin answering the question at what level a NMW should be set we need to turn to the work of Seebohm Rowntree, for, as we have seen in Chapter 3, he was the first person in this country to define carefully what was meant by the term 'poverty'.[1] His aim was to measure the level of income required by families of different sizes so as to provide the minimum of food, clothing and shelter 'needful for the maintenance of mere physical efficiency'.[2] From his very first study Rowntree was anxious that we should understand clearly what was meant by the term 'mere physical efficiency', which he expressed in the following way:[3]

A family living on the scale allowed for in this estimate must never spend a penny on railway fares or omnibus. They must never go into the country unless they walk. They must never purchase a halfpenny newspaper or spend their penny to buy a ticket for a popular concert . . . They cannot save, nor can they join a sick club or trade union, because they cannot pay the necessary subscriptions. The children must have no pocket money for dolls, marbles, or sweets. The father must smoke no tobacco and must drink no beer.

---

[1] For how this compares with Charles Booth's attempt see Frank Field, *Poverty and Politics*, op. cit. chap. 8.

[2] Rowntree, *Poverty: A Study of Town Life*, op. cit., p. 7.

[3] *ibid.*, pp. 133–4.

Using this stringent definition of poverty, Rowntree nevertheless found that large numbers of working families in York had incomes below this poverty level. He estimated that 43 per cent of the wage-earning class, which amounted to 28.8 per cent of the total population of the city, were living in poverty. These findings were similar to those found by Charles Booth from his London surveys,[4] and they helped to fuel the debate about what should be done to counter the wages paid by what were then called the 'sweated trades'.

When this campaign resulted in the then Liberal Government establishing the first trade boards,[5] Rowntree turned his attention to the level at which the minimum wage should be set. For this purpose he argued for a minimum income which was more generous than his poverty line:[6]

We are all agreed that every worker of average ability should receive at least a wage sufficient to maintain him or her in full physical efficiency *and in reasonable comfort* (italics added).

While Rowntree defined his minimum wage in terms of its level being adequate to prevent working families from sinking into poverty, Barbara Wootton reminds us that only in regulations for the Agricultural Wages Board has any attempt been made to lay down officially and explicitly the objectives of minimum wage rates:[7]

The Act of 1924, which first gave the power to fix statutory wages to County Wage Committees, laid down that each Committee should fix such minimum rates in its own area as would 'so far as practicable secure for able-bodied men such wages as in the opinion of the Committee are adequate to promote efficiency and to enable a man in an ordinary case to maintain himself and his family in accordance with such standards of comfort as may be reasonable in relation to the nature of his occupation'.

But this rubric raises as many questions as it answers. To quote Barbara Wootton again:

In what circumstances must it be reckoned frankly 'impracticable' to award a wage that is adequate for efficiency? What is an 'ordinary' case? What size of family is supposed to be dependent upon this able-bodied worker in this

---

[4] Charles Booth, 'The Inhabitants of the Tower Hamlets (School Board Division), Their Condition and Occupations', *JRSS*, Vol. L, 1887, and 'Conditions and Occupations of the People of East London and Hackney 1887', *JRSS*, Vol. LI, 1888.

[5] For details see Frank Field (ed.) *Are Low Wages Inevitable?* (Spokesman Books, 1976) section 3.

[6] Seebohm Rowntree and Frank D. Stuart, *The Responsibility of Women Workers for Dependants* (OUP, 1921) p. 6.

[7] Barbara Wootton, *The Social Foundation of Wages Policy* (Allen & Unwin, 1955) p. 84.

'ordinary' case? Six children? Two children? No children? and – most elusive (and question-begging-question) of all – what is a 'reasonable standard of comfort' and how is this related to the 'nature of a man's occupation'?

Here Barbara Wootton raises some major questions which she herself insists must feature on the agenda of anyone attempting to set a statutory or national minimum wage. But the difficulty of defining what is meant by an ordinary family, as well as answering some of the other questions she poses, has not led to further consideration of what all these different issues might mean in practice; rather it has resulted, in Professor Atkinson's words, in low pay being 'defined in Britain directly in relation to average earnings'. While admitting that this approach 'has no inherent rationale', Atkinson draws out its strengths, for 'it seems to correspond in broad terms to what the survey suggests people generally consider to represent low pay'.[8]

Defining a minimum wage in relation to current earnings also raises a number of questions which need to be answered. What is the correct earnings base? Should it cover all workers, men and women combined, or is it more appropriate to take only the rates paid to male workers, thereby excluding the bias which women workers already face in current wage levels? Is it right to take all occupations, both manual and non-manual, and should overtime earnings be included?

The least satisfactory answer to these questions came from the National Board for Prices and Incomes which in its 1971 Report (p. 1) defined workers as being low-paid if their earnings placed them in the bottom tenth of the relevant earnings league. Such an approach is not very helpful in eliminating low pay, for as long as there are differences in pay there will always be a lowest decile. To meet this criticism, other groups and individuals set a minimum wage target in terms of a set percentage, invariably two-thirds, of median earnings. Writing in their paper for the PSI Conference, Liz Bisset and Emma MacLennan recall that the TUC has now adopted a low-pay definition of two-thirds average earnings[9]:

As with the lowest decile definition, male earnings are used for comparison to eliminate the elements of discrimination and disadvantage inherent in the relative level of female earnings. Unlike the lowest decile, this figure remains fixed relative to the median whatever the expanse of the earnings distribution, and is thus a more consistent measure of low pay.

The Family Incomes Supplement (FIS) was introduced in 1971 as an attempt to bring the low earnings of wage earners with children up to a

[8] A.B. Atkinson, *The Economics of Inequality* (OUP, 1975) p. 112.

[9] *Policies Against Low Pay, op. cit.*, chap. 2.

prescribed minimum which was laid down by the Government. Not unnaturally therefore FIS levels are also used as a way of defining what a minimum wage target should be. Bringing these different low-pay definitions together, we find them giving the following minimum wage targets:

	1982 levels
Family Income Supplement for two-child family	£91.50
Lowest decile male earnings	£89.70
Two-thirds median male earnings	£92.70

Source: 'Low wages in Britain', *Low Pay Review*, 12 February 1983.

This approach of setting a NMW as a proportion of average earnings has one major drawback for those who see a minimum wage as playing an important part in tackling poverty; none of the target figures of around £90 a week (in 1982 figures) guarantees a wage which will break the link between earnings and poverty for the vast majority of workers. The calculations supporting this assertion are set out shortly, but first we need to look again at what has become the more traditional way of setting a target NMW, namely, in relation to the State's own definition of poverty on minimum income, and in doing so we need to consider many of those questions raised earlier by Barbara Wootton.

NMW and poverty

When the issue of low pay re-emerged in trade union circles in the late 1960s, the TUC argued for setting a minimum wage target in terms of the supplementary benefit level for a family with two children. The supplementary benefit scheme provides a minimum income for those unable to work, and the TUC saw an advantage in relating a minimum income target 'to an existing standard of need' which would also 'ensure that a person in work did not receive less than someone drawing supplementary benefits'.[10] We therefore need to consider what gross income is required to give a wage earner the same income as that to which he or she is entitled when unable to work and drawing supplementary benefits.

There are, in fact, four component parts of the supplementary benefit scheme which have a bearing on this question. In the first place, there are the two scale rates, the ordinary and the long-term rate, and we need to discuss which of these is the more appropriate for the purpose in hand. We then have to consider whether the wage will cover one or two adults, whether it will take children into consideration, and

[10] TUC, *Economic Review*, 1969, p. 32.

to what extent and how their needs should be covered. Finally, there is the question of a claimant's rent. We consider each of these different aspects of the supplementary benefit scheme in turn.

First, should the ordinary or long-term scale rate be used as the basis for the calculation? To answer this question we need to look at the rationale behind the two rates of benefit. In 1966, in what was in part an exercise to simplify the rates of benefit, the Government introduced a long-term addition to be paid on top of the ordinary rate of supplementary benefit. Up until that time (and, as it turned out in practice, far beyond it as well) many claimants were paid extra sums to cover special needs. The aim of the reform was 'to remove ... the need to inquire into the day-to-day expenses for which the bulk of discretionary allowances', such as heating and diet, were then paid.[11] Further simplifications followed. In October 1973 the Government introduced a preferential long-term rate for national insurance benefits because:[12]

> people receiving the short-term benefits often return to work within a few weeks and can postpone longer-term requirements – for example, clothes and household equipment – until they are back in employment. Moreover they often have, in addition to the earnings-related supplement for the first six months, deferred wages, holiday pay, income tax refunds, employers' sick pay and other savings to help tide them over their period off work. Those receiving pensions and other long-term benefits are more dependent, however, on the benefit they receive. This in essence is a reason why we felt on this occasion that it was appropriate that those who are dependent on benefit ... for a long period of time, should have a higher level of increase than those on the short term benefit.

At the same time, and for the same reason, the long-term additions to supplementary benefit rates were converted into a long-term rate.

One of the forces in the 1960s and early 1970s behind the campaign for a minimum wage, although not for a statutory minimum, was Jack Jones, the then leader of the Transport and General Workers Union. Debating the level at which the minimum wage should be set, he drew attention to the two different rates of supplementary benefit to argue:[13]

> The long-term rate is specifically aimed at people who are unable to support themselves, and their dependants, for a considerable period of time, and have to rely on the State to meet all their needs. Thus, the long-term rate provides a realistic assessment of what the government sees as the basic minimum needed to support a reasonable living standard.

---

[11] *House of Commons Hansard*, 24 May 1966, 341.

[12] Paul Dean, National Insurance and Supplementary Benefit Bill, Standing Committee Debate (F), 17 May 1973, c. 85.

[13] Jack Jones, *The Case for £30 a Week*, TGWU n.d. p. 3.

A minimum wage will be the earnings on which a considerable number of people have to depend, often for long periods of time. It follows from the reasons presented for establishing the long-term and higher rate of benefit, and the argument put forward by people like Jack Jones, that the long-term supplementary benefit rate should be the basis for calculating at what level a NMW needs to be set if it is to break the link between earnings and poverty.

The second question concerns whose needs should be covered by a NMW. Here we must consider whether the correct basis is for a single person or a two-adult household. How the costs of children are covered is examined later.

There is no one set of data on the number of working households with dependants, although a less than full picture can be built up from a range of different sources. The 1979 GHS, for example, shows 20 per cent of the male labour force as being married, with a non-earning wife and dependent children. To this figure we need to add four other categories of workers: working lone mothers, unemployed husband where the wives are the sole breadwinners, single adult children caring for their frail and often infirm parents, and those households where the presence of a handicapped person prevents one of a two-adult household going out to work. Four per cent of the female workforce are lone parents and 17 per cent of unemployed men have working wives. No exact figures exist on the two other categories of households which the Equal Opportunities Commission groups together as 'carers'. While the EOC estimates that the total number of carers of elderly and handicapped people in the UK is about one and a quarter million, it does not break down this figure between those carers in work and those where the household is totally dependent on benefit, but it may not be unreasonable to assume that half this total will be attempting to work. Adding each of these groups to the total of the male workforce who are single breadwinners we can see that *at any one time*, the number of workers whose earnings have to cover the needs of more than just themselves is considerable. Moreover, as the vast majority of these households have at least two adults dependent on a single wage, and as the objective of a NMW is to break the link between earnings and poverty, it is necessary for the calculations to be based on a two-adult household.

In suggesting that a NMW should cover the needs of two adults as defined by the supplementary benefit scheme, it is important to stress that this line of reasoning runs counter to the increasingly vocal demands amongst some groups of feminists and poverty campaigners for individuals to be viewed as individuals, and not as part of any family or household. We see this line being argued in support of an individually based tax system, as well as for the non-aggregation of resources for the supplementary benefit scheme. Reformers who push these arguments should be aware of where the logic will lead them in respect of the debate over the level at which a minimum wage should be set.

Next, how should the needs of child dependants be included in the calculations for a NMW? For most of this century, Eleanor Rathbone and her successors have campaigned for a system of allowances for children to be paid to all parents – including those in work – and have argued that it is as wrong in principle as it is impracticable to expect any wage system to take account of a worker's family responsibilities. Today the most important single payment for children is child benefit, and the higher the child benefit, the easier it will be to move to an agreement on implementing a NMW. So the question becomes one of what are the costs of children, and to what extent are these needs already met through the benefit system?

Children's needs

At the present time the State defines three sets of payments for children. First, there are the payments under the child benefit scheme, which stood in April 1982 at £5.25 a week for each child. (April 1982 figures are taken in order to make a comparison with the 1982 NES – the latest available.) Secondly, those adults on supplementary benefit who have child dependants claim a range of allowances, depending on the age of their children, as follows:

	£
under 11 –	7.90
11–15 –	11.90
16–17 –	14.30
18+ –	18.60

(These figures *include* the payment of child benefit)

The third system of allowances are paid from the National Insurance Fund for those beneficiaries with children. For claimants on short-term national insurance benefits, such as unemployment and sickness benefit, the weekly allowance for each child was 80p, which was paid in addition to child benefit. For parents drawing the higher rates of national insurance, such as invalidity and widows benefit, the rate for each child paid in addition to their child benefit was £7.70 a week.

Because there are no budgetary studies relating to the absolute and relative costs of meeting the needs of different members of a household, it is impossible to answer the question, 'what is the cost of a child?'

However, it is reasonable to assume that the State would not pay allowances to cover the costs of children which were more generous than it guessed these costs to be. We shall therefore take the cost of a child to be set at the level for the child addition paid to beneficiaries on the higher rates of national insurance benefits.

Following on from this, and because we shall need to look at what the minimum or poverty line income is for a family and then relate this to a gross NMW figure, we need to consider how many children should be included in the calculations. Earlier Barbara Wootton, in relation to the instructions laid down by the 1924 Agricultural Wages Board Act, asked what size should be given to a family dependent on the minimum rate. For purposes of this study we need to see whether there is a size of family which will cover practically all families. The word 'practically' is used for it is obviously possible to choose a number of children which would cover all families – i.e. whatever is the largest family living at the present time in the UK. But such an approach would not only make the implementation of a NMW impracticable; it is also unnecessary. A family with two children covers 'practically' all families; according to the 1981 GHS 82 per cent of families have two or fewer children. The mean number of children per family stood in 1981 at 1.9.[14]

But what of those families with more than two children? How will their minimum needs be covered? The likelihood is that these families will have, on average, older parents. This means that many of these breadwinners will have been in their jobs for a greater length of time than younger workers, and may well have qualified for a higher than basic rate of pay. Moreover, the size of families continues to fall. For those marrying during the 1960–64 period, the average number of children stood at 2.3. The average family size for those marrying during the following five years, 1965–9, stood at 2.[15] While part of this fall may be explained by the time-lag between the marriages of the two groups, the data on the 1965–9 marriages were collected twelve years after the commencement of the study period, and are likely to reflect a genuine, and still further, decline in the size of families which has been apparent for a long period of time. As each year passes these calculations which cover families with two children will become a more, rather than less, accurate reflection of family needs.

Lastly, claimants drawing supplementary benefit have their rents paid in full. Prior to the introduction of a new housing benefit, the weekly benefit gained by SB claimants included money for their rent.

---

[14] *GHS 1981* (HMSO, 1983) Table 2.14.

[15] *ibid.*, Table 2.42.

Since April 1983, claimants on supplementary benefit living in council accommodation have had their rents paid direct. Any NMW, if it is to give a worker a gross income which is at least equal to the income he receives on supplementary benefit, therefore needs to take into account an average rent payment. The latest period on which average rent payments are available is for December 1981, which shows an average weekly rent payment for a non-pensionable household living in council accommodation of £15.25.

Bringing together each of these four stages we can work out the supplementary benefit entitlement for a household with two children in 1982. (The calculations are set out in detail in Appendix 1.) On the assumption that the level of child benefit is not increased above its 1982 level, the weekly supplementary benefit income stands at £78.45. On the assumption of child benefit payments equal to the child additions paid to claimants drawing the higher rate of national insurance benefit, supplementary benefit level entitlement falls to £63.05.

This is itself a major difference. Yet the full effect of including generous child benefit payments in the NMW calculations only becomes apparent once the SB entitlement is reworked into what is called the gross income equivalent – the sum which a worker needs to earn in order to have net pay equal to his SB entitlement. The gross incomes needed to give a net income equal to each of these two levels of income are £102.20 and £76.89 a week respectively. In other words, a NMW which aims to break the link between earnings and poverty would need to be set in 1982 prices at £102.20 a week, if no changes are made to the child benefit system, or at £76.89 a week, if child benefits are paid at the value of the child's addition to the higher rates of national insurance benefit.

Conclusion

This chapter has explored the relationship between a NMW and the adequacy of the child benefit scheme. The demand in 1982 for a £90.00 a week minimum wage has been shown to be inadequate to achieve a wages floor which would break the link between earnings and poverty; also it totally ignores the effect of child benefit payments. A fully developed child benefit scheme makes a major difference to the level at which a NMW needs to be set. We now turn to examining the cost, and to finding out which groups of workers will benefit from a NMW set at the two levels proposed in this chapter.

6 What Costs and Who Benefits?

This chapter begins by examining the cost to the national wages bill of NMWs at £102.20 and £76.89 a week. (So that the NES data can be used, the figures have been rounded to £100.00 and £75.00 respectively.) It looks at which groups of workers would benefit most, and the industries in which they work, before going on to consider what has been predicted as the likely economic impact of any major change in wage levels. The final section reviews some of the research findings on what has been the actual impact on unemployment levels of changing minimum wage rates.

The costs

First we consider who benefits, by what extent, and at what cost to the total wages bill from a NMW which is introduced without any changes in the level of child benefit: in other words, a NMW of £100.00.

At this level, and working from the 1982 NES data, we find that 1.5 million males and 2.7 million females would receive wage increases. Moreover, the wage gap (i.e. the amount of money by which workers fall below the NMW level expressed as a total of the wage bill, and as a percentage of the wage bill) is much greater for women than men.[1] The cost of making up the wage gap for male workers was £23.75m. a week in 1982, or 1.5 per cent of the male wage bill. For female workers it equalled £66.75m. a week, or 14 per cent of the female wage bill. The wage gap for both male and female workers earning below the £100.00 a week mark was equal to 4.4 per cent of the total wage bill of all workers in 1982.

At first glance, 4.4 per cent of a wage bill may not appear such a gigantic sum as to rule a NMW out of court. But in annual terms such a sum equals £4,706m. and this takes no account of any knock-on effect from other workers seeking to re-establish traditional differentials. Moreover, because there is a marked difference in the cost of introducing a NMW for male and female workers, and because wage levels vary both for male and female workers in different industries, it is important also to look at the wage gap on an occupational basis. Again using 1982 data and a £100.00 a week NMW, and referring to the standard occupational groupings, we see from Table 6.1 the number

---

[1] See David Metcalf, *Low Pay, Occupational Mobility and Minimum Wage Policy in Britain* (Centre of Labour Economics, 1980) for an earlier example of this approach.

and percentage of workers in each occupational group whose wage would be affected by the implementation of a NMW at this level.

The table contains information on a number of important points. Many opponents of a NMW strategy claim that such a reform will benefit only the 'pin-money' brigade – their offensive term for female workers. It was stressed earlier that most women go out to work because they are the only breadwinner (they are single or, increasingly, they alone are responsible for dependants) or because their earnings are of crucial importance to their family's finances (see Chapter 3). And while we can see from the table that 2.9 million women workers will gain wage rises from a NMW established at £100.00 a week (this number assumes that no unemployment consequences follow) such a move also benefits 1.8 million males.

A second important issue is also illustrated in the table. While all occupations have some low-paid workers, a few have large numbers earning less than the suggested NMW. The difference is again more pronounced for female than male workers. In only two occupational categories (catering, cleaning, hairdressing and other personal services and farming, fishing and related trades) does the proportion of male workers earning less than a £100.00 a week reach 9 per cent. For female workers, however, 6 occupational groupings (selling, including retailing; catering, cleaning, hairdressing and other personal services; material processing; making and repairing; painting, repetitive assembling, inspecting, packaging and related trades; and transport operating, materials removing and storing trades) out of 18 occupational groups have more than 20 per cent of the workforce earning weekly wage packets of less than £100.00. And in half of these occupations the percentage rises to over 30 per cent.

Obviously a NMW introduced at this level will have a major impact on the economy, particularly through those industries which have large numbers of low-paid workers. But before we look at the employment and other consequences of a NMW set at £100.00 per week, we explore the cost of a lower NMW, accompanied by child benefit payments at £12.95 a week. With child benefit payments at this level, it is possible to set the NMW at £75.00 a week and still ensure that the link between earnings and poverty is broken. With a £75.00 a week NMW, 1.3 million female workers would have gained a pay increase in 1982, as would 0.3 million male workers. The wage gap for female workers would have equalled 3.3 per cent of the female wage bill, or £15.75m. a week, and for males the cost of making good the wage gap would have totalled £2.75m. a week or 0.2 per cent of the male wage bill, the total cost to industry, on an annual basis, amounting to £962m.

A NMW at this level would still have important economic

Table 6.1 The number and percentage of workers, classified by occupation, earning less than £100 a week, April 1982

Occupation Group		Male		Female	
		%	Estimated number earning less than £100 p.w.	%	Estimated number earning less than £100 p.w.
I	General management	n.a.	—	n.a.	—
II	Professional and related supporting management and administration	0.2	31,440	2.8	28,030
III	Professional and related in education, welfare and health	0.6	36,350	4.7	281,630
IV	Literary, artistic and sports	3.1	90,190	6.5	10,850
V	Professional and related in science, engineering technology	0.4	43,020	5.2	25,800
VI	Managerial (excluding general management)	0.9	86,470	10.6	60,260
VII	Clerical and related	2.5	203,980	15.8	1,362,910
VIII	Selling (including retailing)	3.6	105,740	38.7	254,610
IX	Security and protective services	0.6	18,480	1.9	3,230
X	Catering, cleaning, hairdressing and other personal services	9.0	203,800	35.4	401,810

XI	Farming, fishing and related	9.0	114,070	n.a.(a)	—
XII	Material processing (excluding metals)	2.4	69,350	27.7	59,600
XIII	Making and repairing (excluding metal and electrical)	2.3	102,090	32.6	168,770
XIV	Processing, making and related (metal and electrical)	1.0	205,740	11.3	39,450
XV	Painting, repetitive assembling, product inspecting, packaging and related	2.2	85,100	22.7	202,720
XVI	Construction, mining and related	2.3	102,040	n.a.(a)	—
XVII	Transport operating, materials moving and storing	2.8	253,930	20.8	28,310
XVIII	Miscellaneous (including power plant operators and general related)	4.8	50,260	n.a.(a)	—
I–XVIII			1,802,050		2,928,010

Note: (a) Sample size for farming, construction and miscellaneous (mostly general labourers) too small to give an accurate female distribution. Also for general management, both sexes.
Source: *New Earnings Survey 1982*, Part D.

consequences, particularly through those industries characterised by large numbers of female workers. But the objective becomes politically much more realisable than does a NMW without any major child benefit adjustments. Indeed, one is tempted to think that if a minimum wage campaign began to look as though it would be followed through by political action, the CBI and other business groups would be in the forefront of the campaign for adequate family benefits; this would be a very sensible reaction on their part.

These two NMW proposals will have an impact both on employment levels and inflation – though to different degrees. Before we turn in the next chapter to consider the staging mechanism for introducing a NMW, the remainder of this chapter looks at what economists predict will happen if a NMW comes into operation. This is followed by a summary of some of the empirical studies which have surveyed what has actually happened when wage rates have been statutorily raised.

Employment consequences

The major argument which has been put continually against introducing a NMW is its likely impact on the numbers of low-paid who will lose their jobs. The intellectual force behind this argument stems from what is known as the neoclassical school of economics. In all instances this school lays down a clear prediction:[2]

> a raising of wages above the competitive level will contract the demand for labour, and make it impossible to absorb some of the men available. As the employment of labour contracts, the marginal product of the men still employed will rise; when the marginal product has risen to a level corresponding to the new wage, the increase in unemployment will stop.

Put more simply, if wages are raised above those already paid in a competitive market, unemployment will be a consequence.

This neoclassical theory still enjoys a central position in the debate about what can or cannot be done about low pay. The same views are being expressed just as strongly in public debate today, particularly by economists associated with the Institute of Economic Affairs. One IEA campaigner has recently put the neoclassical argument in the following terms:[3]

> The intention of minimum wage laws is to raise the wages of workers at the bottom of the ladder. The actual effect of such legislation has been to cut off the bottom few rungs, thus making it far more difficult for less-skilled workers to obtain jobs for high or even middling pay.

[2] J.R. Hicks, *The Theory of Wages* (Macmillan 1932), p. 1979.

[3] Walter Block, 'Discrimination helps the under privileged', *Journal of Economic Affairs*, July 1982, p. 215.

Of particular concern in the campaign against Britain's limited minimum wage laws has been what is claimed to be the effect of wage council minimum rates on the job prospects of young workers.[4]

Minimum wages, if set above the point at which the market will clear, would deprive the young of their opportunity to price themselves into jobs. Moreover, when labour-market conditions for the young worsen (if, for example, their numbers grow) minimum wages ensure that the maximum adverse effect is inflicted upon this vulnerable group. In a free market, an increased supply of teenagers would cause a fall in their price to enable extra numbers to be absorbed into employment. If the teenage wage remains fixed by legislation, however, no more teenagers can be employed and the extra numbers of teenagers in the population will then simply be reflected in longer employment queues. Minimum wages thus rob the labour market of flexibility to cope with exogenous changes.

This neoclassical stance has not gone unchallenged, although it is important to note what is and is not in dispute. The neoclassical school believes wages are, or rather should be, determined by economic forces alone. Other economists, like Barbara Wootton, emphasise the importance of non-economic forces; to explain the wage and salary structure of Britain 'in purely economic terms . . . is found to be inadequate: such explanations can indeed be made intellectually coherent; but only at the heavy price in the sacrifice of contact with reality'.[5] What is this reality of which Barbara Wootton writes? For her the present wage and salary structure can only be explained in terms of 'the accumulated deposit laid down by a rich mixture of social and economic forces operating through considerable periods of history'.

The reformer is therefore faced with the advice of two groups of economists, both of whom predict economic consequences if a NMW is introduced. Pitching wage rates above the 'clearing level' will lead, according to the neoclassicists, to unemployment. For those economists emphasising the importance of social and conventional forces in wage determination, a NMW may trigger off wage demands in order to re-establish conventional relativities. Both warnings need to be heeded. A NMW set at either of the levels suggested in this study will have detrimental employment effects unless it is phased in over a long enough period, and is accompanied by other countervailing measures. Similarly, a NMW pitched at a high enough level to break the link between earnings and poverty, and which is not accompanied

---

[4] David Forest, 'Minimum wages and youth unemployment. Would Britain learn from Canada?', *Journal of Economic Affairs*, July 1982, p. 249.

[5] Wootton, *op. cit.*, p. 161.

by an agreed incomes policy, is likely to trigger off wage demands so as to re-establish traditional relativities. Both these points are important at a time of high unemployment, and particularly when the electorate has shown itself prepared to allow unemployment to rise in order to control inflation. We shall return to both of these themes in the following chapter. First, however, because the employment consequences of a NMW are likely to feature prominently in any subsequent campaign (see, for example, the articles and letters in *The Guardian* during August 1983), the final section of this chapter reviews some of the main research findings on the impact on employment of NMW changes.

Empirical results

As the papers at the PSI Conference make clear, most of the studies bearing on the impact of minimum wage legislation on employment levels have been carried out in the United States and Canada. Details of each of these major pieces of work are given in the appendix to Mary Eccles's paper at the PSI Conference.[6] Here a summary is given based on the OECD review of minimum wage studies carried out in the US and Canada since 1970.[7] The OECD cited one review of 13 research studies which concluded:

there is no convincing evidence to refute the prediction that minimum wages cause reductions of employment (for young workers at least).

Likewise, a review conducted for the American Minimum Wage Study Commission of changes in the level of teenage employment found 'on average a 10 per cent increase in the minimum wage reduces teenage employment between 0.5 and 3 per cent', although it is true to say that most of these studies showed employment affected over the narrower range of between 1 and 2.5 per cent. Taking this lower estimate, the OECD review concluded:

It appears that on average a 10 per cent rise in the minimum wage would result in a decline in teenage employment of about 1 per cent.

This has led some economists and politicians to propose a special youth minimum wage rate. The main effect of such a proposal is to lessen the impact on costs of increased wages, and, at the same time, to place younger workers in a more attractive employment position than some older workers. While there is only a limited literature on the effects of a youth minimum wage, work carried out for the Minimum

---

[6] *Policies Against Low Pay, op. cit.*

[7] *OECD Observer*, No. 117, July 1982.

Wage Study Commission suggested that teenage employment would increase by about 3 per cent if a 25 per cent youth differential was established. The Commission reported in the following terms:[8]

A reasonable prediction might be that teenage employment would increase by 1.5 to 3 per cent in response to a 15 per cent differential, and by 2.5 to 5 per cent in response to a 25 per cent differential, but there is no substantial certainty that the true effect would be within that range. Adult unemployment would probably be reduced, but it is very unlikely that the adult employment reductions would be as large as teenage employment gains.

In France, while the number of studies on the impact of SMIC is far fewer than those carried out on the effect of the US minimum wage – a point which applies to all the country studies at the PSI Conference – the effect of changes in SMIC is nevertheless disputed. Véronique Sandavall reports in her paper on one recent study claiming to explain the variations in teenage unemployment over the period between 1968 and 1977 by means of changes in the French minimum wage rate. But other work, looking at the unemployment rate of young people and their activity rate over the last two decades, reaches the opposite conclusion.[9]

An OECD report looking at the effect of minimum wage changes in both France and the US concluded[10]

that evidence of significant disemployment effects for French youths arising from changes in the SMIC could not be found with any precision from time-data series data on French youth employment over the past two decades. This is in contrast to the typical findings in the vast North American literature which shows that increases in the level and coverage of the minimum wage have led to small, but nevertheless significant, job losses among teenagers.

Even less research has been carried out on the employment effects of the Australian arbitration system. Duncan MacDonald's contribution to the PSI Conference papers[11] draws attention to the extent of studies on the working of the arbitration system although, with one exception, the impact on employment of the minimum wage has escaped the attention of researchers. This single exception concluded that if the Australian Arbitration Commission were to maintain the rate of increase in the minimum wage to that prescribed between 1966 and 1972,

---

[8] *ibid.*

[9] *Policies Against Low Pay, op. cit.*, chap. 6.

[10] 'The Impact of minimum wages on young people's jobs: The French experience', *OECD Observer*, No. 118, September 1982.

[11] *Policies Against Low Pay, op. cit.*, chap. 7.

then employment opportunities would be decreased for marginal workers.

What of Britain? There have been no recent studies carried out on the impact of the minimum rates laid down by wages councils. This was, however, a topic which was researched carefully by R.H. Tawney and his colleagues when the first minimum rates were set back in 1909. Detailed studies were carried out on the impact of the minimum wage on employment in three of the four industries covered. In the chain-making industry:[12]

> enquiries both among workers and employers show that there has been no decrease in the numbers employed. On the contrary, the general statement of both is that more are employed than at any previous time.

The same is true of the other two trades about which we have detailed knowledge. M.E. Bulkley, reporting on the effect of minimum wages on employment in the box-making industry, wrote that, while a certain number of adult workers had been dismissed, 'it appears that anything like unemployment on a serious scale . . . isn't likely to take place in the future.'[13]

Tawney reported in a similar fashion on the effect of the minimum wage on employment opportunities in the tailoring industry. Very few people were made unemployed when the minimum rates came into effect. Tawney believed, however, that the minimum wage would affect recruitment. He estimated that new workers would be taken on less frequently, partly because the effect of the increase in wages had been to increase the output of firms without a corresponding increase in the labour force, partly because it was no longer so profitable to employ cheap juvenile labour. He concluded by adding:[14]

> But since the trade is constantly growing there is no reason to anticipate any considerable unemployment of workers who are already in the trade.

Too much stress should not be placed on these results; they have been cited here because they constitute the only detailed research – as opposed to assertions – on what occurred in this country when a government set out to raise by law the wages of some groups of very low-paid workers. But the world in which Tawney researched has since seen two world wars and an inflation on the scale equal only to that

[12] R.H. Tawney, *The Establishment of Minimum Rates in the Chain Making Industry* (Bell, 1913) p. 106.

[13] M.E. Bulkley, *The Establishment of Legal Minimum Rates in the Box Making Industry* (Bell, 1915), p. 63.

[14] R.H. Tawney, *The Establishment of Minimum Rates in the Tailoring Industry* (Bell, 1915), pp. 181–2.

which followed the Tudor debasement of the currency. Moreover, the balance in using capital and labour is now very different from that operating seventy years ago. And there is one other major difference which needs to be stressed. Tawney's world was one where full employment was unknown; indeed the word 'unemployment' had only entered the language of political economists when it was used by Alfred Marshall in 1883.[15] Making a major increase in a worker's standard of living by way of a minimum wage at a time when there were effectively no welfare benefits for workers to supplement inadequate wages, and when full employment was unknown, is a very different proposition from now, when unemployment is seen by the electorate as the prime domestic issue. Increases in unemployment – if only marginal – need to be taken seriously, and part of the whole packet of measures which needs to accompany any introduction of a NMW are compensatory ones which will protect the position of vulnerable workers.

Work in progress at the Henley Centre for Forecasting makes it possible to be more precise about the likely effects of a NMW on employment levels. (I am indebted to Paul Ormerod at the Henley Centre for this information.) The Henley Centre's work suggests that, for manufacturing, a 1 per cent rise in labour costs decreases manufacturing employment by 0.3 per cent. As we saw earlier, a NMW of £100.00 a week in 1982 is likely to increase male and female labour costs by 1.5 per cent and 14 per cent respectively, or by 4.4 per cent overall. Assuming that the relationship of changes in manufacturing labour costs to employment levels holds throughout the economy, the Henley Centre's forecast suggests a NMW at £100.00 a week will decrease total employment by around 1.5 per cent and women's employment by around 4.5 per cent. Because there are different proportions of men and women in the labour force, it is not valid to average the change in female and male employment. However, for women workers alone the reduction in employment would be in the region of 405,000 jobs.

These employment consequences of implementing a NMW are serious, but if the trade union movement decided on a policy of re-establishing differentials, the effects would be little short of disastrous. To say this is not to argue against a NMW; rather it is to emphasise the need to work out a programme of compensatory measures to introduce simultaneously with the introduction of a NMW.

It is also necessary to face squarely the question of the 'cost' of a minimum wage. Any programme of compensatory measures to minimise the employment effects is likely to involve calls upon public expenditure. These calls upon the public purse will mean less expend-

---

[15] José Harris, *Unemployment and Politics* (OUP, 1972), p. 4.

iture elsewhere, or higher public expenditure matched by lower personal consumption. (The other option would be for a government to borrow to finance any compensatory programme, but there are clearly limits to this option as any radical government will be concerned not to push up interest rates too high.) The introduction of a NMW has to be balanced, therefore, against the postponement of, say, introducing a disability income scheme, or a cut-back in the hospital or home-building programme. Again it is important that advocates of a NMW strategy help the public to face up to the obvious but important truth that this option for helping the low-paid – like all others – cannot be done without someone being asked to foot the bill.

The cost of introducing a NMW has to be borne in another way too. The conclusion among economists is that a £100.00 a week minimum wage would initially raise prices by 2 to 2.5 per cent unless there are corresponding increases in productivity to offset the higher labour costs. If the economic repercussions of introducing a minimum wage are to be limited, therefore, this rise in prices will have to be borne by wage and benefit holders without any, or with only limited, compensatory changes. In this sense, therefore, wage earners and others will be helping to finance the cost of a NMW and this will take the form of a cut of up to 2.5 per cent in real living standards. Again, this is not a reason necessarily against introducing a national minimum wage; rather it underlines the importance of thinking through properly the full costs of the strategy.

Conclusion

In this chapter we have examined which groups of workers would benefit from the introduction of a minimum wage; with either a £75.00 or a £100.00 a week NMW substantial numbers of workers will benefit, although obviously more gain at the higher level. The discussion has also been concerned with the likely economic consequences of such a move. Evidence from US studies shows that a relatively minor increase in the minimum wage is associated with a small, but not unimportant, rise in unemployment. The size of the change in wage rates proposed in this book and elsewhere is far in excess of the changes considered in these studies, and by implication the employment consequences must be similarly greater. Indeed, the provisional estimates considered above suggest not only a sizeable reduction in employment levels with a minimum wage at £100.00 a week, but that any general policy to re-establish differentials will have disastrous employment consequences. Again, this is not a reason for not introducing a minimum wage, but rather to emphasise the importance of winning widespread public support for it, while at the same time introducing a strategy to mitigate any employment consequences. It is to this issue that we now turn.

7 A Programme of Compensatory Measures

A NMW set at a level generous enough to prevent working families from being poor would have two important economic repercussions: on employment levels and on the rate of inflation. This chapter outlines those measures which will be necessary to counter these two effects, and begins by setting out the argument for bringing in any NMW over a fairly lengthy time period. As part of this staging progress, the case is presented for a junior minimum wage rate. This is followed by a discussion of the reasons why a minimum wage strategy needs to be accompanied by an incomes policy. The chapter concludes by considering the scope and role of manpower and investment policies which also need to make up part of a successful minimum wage strategy.

Employment effects

We saw in the previous chapter that the effect on the total wage bill of implementing a NMW at £75.00 a week in 1982 was fairly modest, amounting to a 0.9 per cent increase. A somewhat different picture emerged if the impact was divided between the male and female wages bill. While a NMW of £75.00 a week would add only 0.2 per cent to industry's bill for male employment, it would increase the costs of employing female workers by a total of 3.3 per cent. The cost is massively greater if the NMW is introduced without the full development of the child benefit scheme; a NMW of £100.00 a week is then required. Set at this level, the minimum wage would add 4.4 per cent to industry's costs for employing male workers and 14 per cent for female workers.

But even these figures under-estimate the impact of a NMW. A £100.00 a week NMW would require the *doubling* of the wages of 100,000 women workers – the group shown to be earning £50.00 or less in 1982 – and almost doubling the wages of a further 300,000 workers earning between £50.00 and £55.00 a week. Even with a minimum wage of £75.00 a week we are talking of increasing the wage costs of employing these workers by around 50 per cent. And as we have seen, many of the lowest paid are heavily concentrated in a narrow band of employment. Any minimum wage strategy therefore needs to be considered in stages. That is true even of one accompanied by high child benefit payments, although the time span would of course be considerably less. What kind of timetable is envisaged?

The idea of staging the full introduction of a major measure like a NMW is not new. When the Equal Pay Act was given a legislative basis there was no disagreement over the need to allow a longish period of time for firms to begin adjusting to its terms. The EPA went on to the statute book in 1970, but was not brought into operation until December 1975 – six years later. Chapter 10 gives details of how women's pay altered as a percentage of men's pay over this period. The total effect was for the female wage bill to rise by 17.5 per cent. A NMW not accompanied by a full child benefit scheme would increase women's pay by less than this amount: by 14 per cent. If employment conditions were as favourable now as they were in the early 1970s, this would suggest a timetable of around 4–5 years as a minimum for bringing this proposal into full effect. A time scale of 5 years is proposed here, but as present employment conditions are far less favourable, it is also important to consider other staging mechanisms.

A second such phasing-in proposal is for the simultaneous introduction of a junior minimum wage rate. Generally speaking, the wages of younger workers are lower than those of other workers. A NMW which immediately covers all workers will have a greater impact on employment levels than one which operates fully only above a certain age limit.

Can the move to introduce a junior minimum wage be justified? It may be attacked by those (rightly) campaigning for a better deal for younger workers. But the logic of a junior minimum wage derives directly from the objectives of a minimum wage strategy as defined in this study. The rate was set at a level to prevent an average-size family dependent on one wage being poor. Clearly such conditions do not apply to the overwhelming majority of young workers.

There are two additional reasons why careful consideration should be given to the idea of a junior minimum wage. First, the relative pay rates for younger workers have risen appreciably since the early 1970s. One set of figures show the average gross weekly earnings of full-time employees under the age of 21, as a percentage of the corresponding figure for those aged 21 and over, rising from 46 per cent in 1973 to 54 per cent in 1980.[1] While there has been a heated debate on whether these figures account for the disproportionate rise in youth unemployment, or whether the increase can be explained in terms of the large influx of younger workers on to the labour market, the latest research study is not supportive of those who minimise the employment effects of large increases in pay, particularly in the short run.

[1] *House of Commons Hansard*, 13 July 1983, 268–9.

This study, conducted by the Department of Employment, concentrated on the 1969–81 period; the report stresses that previously DE research had not detected any significant effect of relevant youth pay upon employment but this was because it concentrated on an earlier period.[2] In contrast this latest study found:[3]

> Employment of under 18 year olds of both sexes seems to have suffered quite appreciably because of their increased relative labour costs. The results for males under 18 show that a one per cent change in earnings of males under 21 relative to males 21 and over is associated with the fall in employment of males under 18 of at least two per cent. Significant decreases in employment are also associated with increase in earnings relative to both adult and youth females.

Secondly, as we saw in the previous chapter, most of the research on the effects of minimum wage increases on employment levels has been carried out in the United States. Here it was found that an increase in the minimum was associated with small, but not unimportant, increases in unemployment. Currently the US minimum rate stands at 42 per cent of average earnings, although it is true that, of late, the rate has fallen in relative terms as its last revision was back in 1981. Even so, as Mary Eccles shows, the value of the American minimum wage as compared with earnings has never risen above its 1968 level of 53 per cent of average earnings.[4] Minimum wage demands in the UK, when not accompanied by a major boost to the child benefit scheme, put the wage at two-thirds average earnings. This is a significant difference compared with the American scene, and the employment consequences of attempting to introduce a NMW – even over a fairly long time-scale – which has this as a target level, are likely to be substantial. Hence the case for a junior minimum wage, at least during the early stages of the policy, and particularly so if the minimum wage is not accompanied by commensurate increases in child benefit.

Before selecting the age at which the junior minimum wage ceases to operate and the full NMW comes into effect, we need to look at the age when first children are born. The age of the father is taken, as it will be the father – at least in the early stages of the family's life – who is more likely to be the breadwinner. The only data to hand are those compiled by the Office of Population, Census and Surveys. These show that, while in 1980 5.9 per cent of legitimate live births were to fathers under 20, there have been two trends at work in recent years. In respect of

---

[2] See, for example, P.D.J. Makeham, *Youth Unemployment*, DE research paper 10, 1980.

[3] W. Wells, 'Relative pay and employment of young people', *Employment Gazette*, June 1983 p. 237.

[4] See chapter 5, *Policies Against Low Pay, op. cit.*

legitimate paternities, the total number of fathers under 20 has been falling (down from 13,065 in 1975 to 9,889 in 1980) and that the number of very young fathers is simultaneously decreasing.[5]

After the age of 19 the number of legitimate paternities begins to increase rapidly. While we have just seen that the total number of such paternities for all age groups up to 19 years stood at 9,889 in 1980, the number of legitimate paternities for 20 year old males was 10,947, rising further to 16,388 for 21 year olds, and the rate continues to rise up to and including fathers aged 27. The figures would suggest therefore that any junior minimum rate should cease at a worker's 20th birthday. But again it must be stressed that a junior minimum wage follows directly from what is taken here to be the minimum wage's main function, namely, to ensure an income for a single-wage household which is generous enough to break the link between earnings and poverty. Any minimum wage act should lay down a mechanism for regularly reviewing the progress made under the act, and part of any such review would be of the junior rate. How long a junior rate will be necessary will depend on the extent to which the child benefit scheme has adequate funds channelled into it. The higher the child benefit payments, the smaller will be the difference between the two levels of minimum wages discussed in this book i.e. around £75.00 and £100.00 a week. The nearer the child benefit payments take the minimum wage towards the £75.00 mark, the less need there will be for a junior minimum wage.

Inflationary effects

Because the inflationary effects of introducing a NMW will be more widely spread, they will be easier to compensate for than the employment effects. We have already seen that the likely increases in the total wages bill for a NMW of £75.00 a week and £100.00 a week are 0.9 and 4.4 per cent respectively. Again, taking the Henley Centre's forecast of the rise in prices for each 1 per cent in labour costs, we find a £100.00 NMW resulting in a 2 to 2.5 per cent rise in prices. But just as the impact of a NMW is not evenly spread throughout the economy, so too there will be a differential impact on costs and prices. The inflationary impact will be concentrated most heavily on the prices of those goods and services produced by today's labour-intensive and/or low-wage industries.

There is a case for arguing that, as a NMW is seen as a move supported by large sections of the electorate (and if not, it is unlikely to be successful), in order to remedy the evil of people earning low wages,

---

[5] OPCS birth statistics, FM 1/7, 1980, table 11.1.

the community should be prepared to help shoulder the cost. This can be achieved in a number of ways. Employers may bear the whole cost. They may try and share the cost by passing on much of their increased labour costs in increased prices. Any rise in prices might be offset by the payment of short-term subsidies by the Government, or the joint payment of subsidies from the Government and the trade union movement.

In the PSI Conference volume, *Policies Against Low Pay*, we saw how the Norwegian trade unions levy their membership in order to finance half the cost of industry implementing the trade unions' demand for a low-pay guarantee. A similar approach could be adopted here by the trade unions (how this fund should be organised is looked at in the following chapter). But, however these payments are financed, and whichever organisation makes such payments, the subsidy should be for a limited period of time only; its aim is to facilitate the transition to a higher paid, more efficient economy, not to facilitate a new lease of life for low-paid employment.

Incomes policy

It is unlikely that a NMW would be introduced other than by a government which was also attempting to move back towards full employment. This move alone will need to be accompanied by some form of incomes policy if any reflation of the economy is not to find its way into higher prices and increased imports. An incomes policy is also a necessary accompaniment for a NMW policy. What little evidence there is of public attitude shows it to be favourable; a poll in *The Guardian* of 7 September 1982 reported that 85 per cent of respondents said they were in favour of a minimum wage. Similar support is shown for an incomes policy.

This support needs to be built upon and developed so that the public, and particularly those at work, see the reasons why an incomes policy is a necessary part of a NMW strategy. It would be nice to plan for the cost of a NMW coming from profit margins. The truth is that in some instances profit margins are too low and any growth in employment will require an increase in profits (although this does not necessarily mean profits rising as a share of national income). Yet an effective incomes policy does mean that some firms will pay less than they would otherwise settle for, and proposals need to be put forward on how to share any additional gains accruing to the corporate sector as a result of this aspect of incomes policy. But, as a minimum wage is about redistributing that part of national income which goes to wages and salaries, it is important not to pull punches on this point. No attempt should be made to sell a minimum wage to the trade unions, or to anyone else, on the basis that it will provide a launching pad from which other workers can win equivalent or even greater increases in wages.

This is a real danger. In an attempt to gain a wider basis for approval within the TUC, NUPE's Deputy General Secretary has declared:[6]

> In addition to protecting the weak and giving the unions a new appeal to low-paid workers, a statutory minimum wage *could also be used as a base for the more powerful bargaining groups who could use it as a springboard for their proper place in the earning league* (italics added).

What form should an incomes policy take? This is not the place to spell out the details of how an incomes policy might work, although it is important for this task to be undertaken at an early opportunity; incomes policies in the past have been cobbled together in great haste with 'help for the low-paid' assuming the role of a last-minute fig leaf, rather than a central goal for the whole strategy.[7]

Any policy which is going to have a chance of longer-term success will need to cover the following issues. First, there will be a need for an incomes policy to be set within the wider context of what the Government hopes to achieve on the economic front over a rolling five-year period. Second, it will be important to state what level of total wage and salary increases is consistent with the Government's overall objectives on the level of employment and rate of inflation. Third, within the total earnings increase discussion will need to take place on how much can be devoted to achieving the yearly staged introduction of a NMW and what proportion will need to go to more general wage and salary increases. Fourth, it is necessary to debate the machinery by which an incomes policy is to be run. Will it be a purely government affair or will other parties – Parliament, employers, unions and consumer groups – be involved in debating both the broader economic strategy within which incomes policy has its place, and the more specific questions relating to wage and salary levels at any given time? Fifth, there will be a need within this newly established machinery to deal with the perceived injustices which are thrown up by any incomes policy which lasts more than a year or two.

There is an urgent need to begin early in the present Parliament a dialogue within centre-left radical and trade union circles on these issues. Such early discussions – which should include as many interested parties as possible – will have two major advantages. They will help to win a greater public understanding about the objectives of the

---

[6] Tom Sawyer, *Tribune*, 3 September 1982.

[7] See Charles Carter and John Pinder, *Policies for a Constrained Economy* (Heinemann, 1982) for a discussion on how widely drawn an incomes and prices policy will need to be.

policy and what this will mean in a year by year wage bargaining process. Such a public debate will also help to highlight some of the banana skins which litter the way of most human activities, but which seemingly have a special attraction for the path of those trying to tread an incomes policy.

Manpower and investment policy

While there is also the need to implement a range of policies concerned with raising the productivity of low-paid workers, these should not be seen in isolation; if they are to be successful they need to be part of a wider strategy to raise productivity generally throughout the economy. Raising productivity requires higher investment levels in many areas, this investment being fully utilised, and the level of skill in the workforce rising commensurately. As the previous section makes clear, one aim of an incomes policy is to increase the resources available for investment, and part of 'selling' an incomes policy ought to be the opening up of a debate on who should own this new investment which has been 'paid for' by workers holding back on wage demands. (Viewed in this light, an incomes policy offers the opportunity to begin planning ways of spreading the ownership of capital amongst the workforce.) But any new investment needs to be utilised fully, and failure to do so is not always the workers' fault. A Clothing Economic Development Council report[8] concluded that the output of the seven firms studied could have been raised by between 26 and 142 per cent; the main reason for not realising this potential productivity increase was a failure of management to control excess costs.

While it is true that some low-paid sectors, like agriculture, are characterised by high levels of investment and complemented by a very skilled labour force, this is not true of most low-paid sectors. Indeed, if it were true, a policy of raising the wages of the low-paid could be a fairly quick and painless operation. Two questions therefore immediately arise: in low-paid sectors, where is the investment to come from, and how are the skills of the workforce to be increased?

As one aspect of a general incomes policy will be to favour the low-paid, it will be in those industries where it is most necessary to raise investment that the greatest pressure will be found to squeeze profit margins in order to meet the enlarged wages bill. How can this apparent circle be squared? One proposal which is made in the following section is for the trade unions to begin financing through a levy system on all workers part of the immediate cost of raising the wages of the lowest-paid. Government assistance will also be needed. But any such aid,

[8] Clothing EDC, *Unlocking Productivity Potential*, 1975.

either from taxpayers, or through a trade union levy, should not be used to give low-paid industries a longer life as low payers. Any help must be linked to structural changes in the industry, and here the NEDC sector working parties could play a crucial role. Long-term plans on investment levels, pay and productivity need to be agreed within each of the major low-paying sectors. At the start of these intra-industrial sector discussions the Government should make clear what it is prepared to offer in terms of both investment finance and training resources.

Increased investment in low-paying industries should be seen as only part of a wider programme of industrial regeneration. Skill levels also need to be increased to match improved investment programmes and to this end an attempt should be made to begin building a national training programme out of the current series of special employment measures which has been announced over the years since 1975. While a great deal of emphasis has been placed on the training aspect of each of these initiatives, their immediate purpose has been to reduce the numbers on the dole. This is not to say that the measures have not been beneficial; they have, for example, made some trainees employable. Anyone interviewing trainers and trainees knows that one of the biggest claims for these courses is that they are successful in giving trainees a grounding in basic educational skills. But the more the claims of success are based on teaching the 3 'R's, the greater becomes the question of what is going on in schools when, after eleven years of State investment, many young people leave hardly able to read or write. There is a need, therefore, to link any proposals for increased training with changes in secondary schooling.

The school-leaving age is now 16 and the vast majority of young people then move into the labour market and seek work. Of those who are successful in gaining work, the vast majority go to jobs which have little training attached to them. This is in stark contrast to what happens in those countries which are our major competitors. Table 7.1 gives the distribution of young people in work, education and training in some of the countries competing with us in the world market. While it relates to the 1976–8 period, there is no evidence to show that the pattern of employment, education and training has altered since then.

What has changed, however, since the table was drawn up is the growth in the UK Government's employment and training programmes, the latest of which goes under the title of the Youth Training Scheme. The YTS started on 1 April 1983 and became fully operative by September 1983. It replaces previous schemes, such as the Youth Opportunities Scheme, and whereas YOP was seen as a temporary measure, providing mainly six-month courses of work experience and work preparation, it is claimed that the YTS provides a high-quality

Table 7.1 Activities of young people after compulsory school period

Country	Year	Ages of compulsory schooling	Full Time Education	Vocational Training/Education	Employment/ Unemployment	Other/ Unknown
EEC Countries						
Belgium	1977	6–14	55	40	4	1
Denmark	1976	7–16	23	43	31	3
W. Germany	1976	6–15	21	69	9	1
France	1978	6–16	27	54	19	–
Ireland	1977	6–15	56	15	29	–
Italy	1977	6–14	20	54	23	3
Luxembourg	1977	6–15	31	54	15	–
Netherlands	1976	6–16	35	38	26	1
United Kingdom	1977	5–15	32	24	44	–

Sources: UNESCO, *1981 Statistical Yearbook*, Table 3.1.
OECD, *Policies for Apprenticeship*, 1979, Table 3.
Second Report of the Education, Science and Arts Committee HC 116–1, 1981/82, pp. cxi–cxv.
MSC, *Outlook on Training*.

integrated programme of training and planned work experience lasting up to a year. It is designed to give school-leavers a range of practical transferable skills to enable them to compete more effectively in the labour market.

There is a need to develop the scheme in a much more radical way so that it becomes the basis of a national training and manpower programme. Such a programme should begin during secondary schooling and continue initially for at least two years after the statutory school-leaving age. If the programme is to be a success, one necessary ingredient is to involve employers in the planning and operation of the scheme. As Charles Carter and John Pinder make only too clear in their recent work,[9] part of the reinforcing bias against industry in this country stems from an education system which employs educators who have by and large had very little experience of earning any other living, let alone working in industry or commerce. Employers, trade unionists and employee associations need to be involved in designing both secondary school syllabuses in general and the syllabuses and the running of post-16 training courses in particular.

One aim of the training programme will be to raise the skill level of the actual and potential working population, and thus to lessen the supply of unskilled labour for low-paid jobs. But help is also needed for those who are currently in low-paid work; new training initiatives need to be designed so that the existing labour force can adapt easily to changes in investment, as well as training for jobs outside currently low-paid occupations.

Some low-paid jobs will be less open to improvements in productivity. Agriculture is already highly productive and the manpower highly skilled; in this sector it is much more a question of the political will to raise wages than anything else. This is not true, of course, in most low-paying sectors; indeed, in some there is no painless way of increasing the pay of the poorest workers. While increases in investment and productivity have a crucial part to play in any strategy against low pay, it is also important to face squarely the issue that any programme to eradicate low pay will, in some instances, involve consumers paying prices which allow the payment of decent wages. And, as with all Britain's economic and industrial problems, it will be easy to get this message across if the economy is growing, more jobs are being created, and living standards generally are improving.

Conclusion

This chapter has been concerned with examining the range of com-

---

[9] Carter and Pinder, *op. cit.*

pensatory measures which will need to accompany the introduction of a NMW. It has been argued that there will be both employment and inflationary consequences of implementing a minimum wage, although the consequences on both these fronts will be that much less if the minimum wage is accompanied by a major injection of funds into the child benefit scheme. If there are no such child benefit adjustments, it will be necessary to phase in the minimum wage over a number of years; a five-year time span is suggested here. It has also been suggested that, as at least part of the staging mechanism, a junior minimum wage should be introduced. As a minimum wage will also have an effect on inflation, although the impact will be much smaller than on the employment front, the discussion has turned to ways of minimising this side-effect. So that differentials are not re-established — and for other reasons — this chapter also argued the need for a minimum wage to be accompanied by an incomes policy. In addition, it is important to raise investment and productivity levels in those low-paying sectors where this is a practicable possibility.

8 The Trade Unions' Response

While trade unions readily see the advantages which the law gives them for carrying out their work, the union movement has a long history of opposing State intervention in what is termed 'free collective bargaining'. This chapter examines the trade union response to the challenge of low pay, in the wages council sector in particular, before going on to outline what the basis is of a trade union alternative to a statutory minimum wage.

Early period
Low pay did not feature in any political debates during the period immediately after the Second World War. One reason for this omission was, no doubt, the lack of any comprehensive information on earnings. The first post-war earnings survey did not take place until 1960, and these data were not used until 1967 when Judith Marquand attempted to sketch in the main dimensions of low earnings.[1] Alan Fisher and Bernard Dix, writing in 1974 when they were the General Secretary and the Research Officer of NUPE respectively, could not therefore be accused of an under-estimation when they remarked on the slow trade union response to the issue of low pay.[2]

During the early part of the 1960s the trade union movement in total, as identified by the TUC, gave little or no attention to the problems of low pay as such.

Fisher and Dix view this period as 'a missed opportunity', citing in support the 1963 General Council's report, *Economic Development and Planning*, which failed even to mention the issue of low pay, let alone propose any remedial actions. But this report did stress one line of thinking which we shall need to recall later in this discussion. It posed the questions:[3]

Can collective bargaining machinery be used to secure a more just and equitable distribution of personal income, which would involve trade unionists in taking account of the effects of their action on fellow trade unionists in other industries? To what extent and how can trade unionists influence such national objectives as . . . the redistribution of the nation's wealth?

[1] J. Marquand, 'Which are the low-paid workers?', *British Journal of Industrial Relations*, Vol. 5, 1976, pp. 359–74.

[2] Alan Fisher and Bernard Dix, *Low Pay and how to end it* (Pitman, 1974), p. 17.

[3] TUC *Report*, 1963, p. 494.

The early 1960s were, in fact, marked by discussions on a second phase of incomes policy. (The first round of modern incomes policy was imposed at the end of the Attlee Government's period of office; the 1930s had been characterised by an 'incomes policy' which had controlled wage and salary rises by the level of unemployment). Fisher and Dix maintain (p. 19) that, during these 'crucial formative debates' within the trade unions and Labour Party,

there was little recognition of the vital need to build into the general policies a specific element designed to solve the particular problem of the low-paid section of the working class.

The blame for this omission is not put squarely at the door of the Labour movement. By the use of Byzantine logic the two trade unionists are able to conclude (p. 20):

The initial blame . . . must rest with the Conservative Government and its allies. With their political advertising campaign to sell the affluent society they had created a market for the product and in the process had blunted the sensibilities of the country to the fact that there were many workers who were too low paid to qualify for entry into that market.

A serious trade union response to the issue of low pay only began to emerge under the pressures of a Labour Government's incomes policy, and this occurred late in 1965. Even so, the initial reactions went little beyond the General Council blandly asserting that the Government's incomes policy 'must take account of the need to promote social equity, in particular to protect groups of very low-paid workers'.[4]

Yet it was in these early debates that we can see the two main alternative courses of action which have later dominated the trade union debate on low pay. At the 1966 TUC Congress the G & M leader – Lord Cooper – told delegates[5]

Unless it is accepted that the problem should be dealt with by a national minimum wage, which must be at least considered as a possibility, the primary responsibility for securing preferential treatment for low-paid workers in private industry must rest on the trade unions themselves.

Trade unions chose – if they made any choice at all – to adopt the second alternative put by the G & M. But it was not until the TUC's 1968 *Economic Review* that the details of this policy began to emerge. In essence, the approach was for trade unions to seek 'to establish a £15.00 minimum earnings guarantee' for a 40-hour week for adult males. Female earnings were so far behind those of their male colleagues that the unions accepted the need for a two-stage policy. Moreover, an

[4] TUC *Report*, 1966, p. 326.

[5] *ibid.*, p. 463.

earnings guarantee was sought rather than a commitment to raise all basic rates to £15.00 because, taking into account the effect that this would have on differentials and earnings, such a demand 'would have a major inflationary effect' (p. 69). The report went on to outline what this policy entailed:

It would involve (*a*) the General Council seeking to secure from the CBI their broad agreement to the objective and their agreement to recommend it to employers' associations; (*b*) negotiations at the level of particular industries between unions and employers, and possibly the establishment of joint teams to examine what improvements can be made in organisation, in the use of labour, and in wages structure with the specific aim of raising the productivity and earnings of lower paid workers: the timing of the achievement of the objective might vary from one industry to another; (*c*) discussions with the Government about the help that it can give in promoting this objective; one type of assistance might be Government action on a selective basis to promote development in areas characterised by low earnings, and achievement of the objective might also involve enforcement action at a later stage at least in some industries.

And this essentially has been the official trade union response to low pay ever since. While the approach to the CBI proved disappointing, and discussions with the Government fared little better, the TUC made no attempt to revise its strategy. On occasions individual trade unions have made demands for a statutory approach but, as we shall see later, this has not yet commanded majority support. The emphasis has been instead on a collective bargaining approach as the means of tackling low pay.

In Chapter 1 we saw that one of the largest concentrations of low-paid workers is to be found in the wages council sector. It is this sector which was (and is) most in need of a policy to tackle low pay and so provide the TUC's strategy with its most obvious chance of success. We need, therefore, to turn now and examine how effective the trade unions' approach of strengthening free collective bargaining has been in tackling low pay in this sector. How well have trade union aspirations been matched by positive results?

Wages council sector

To begin answering this question we need to turn to the Royal Commission on Industrial Relations chaired by Lord Donovan. Established in 1965, its Report was presented to Parliament in the middle of 1968. As part of its remit the Commission examined the wages council sector, and its approach followed very much the official trade union line.

The Commission proposed four main measures to encourage the development of voluntary collective bargaining machinery in the wages council sector. These were to allow a trade union to apply unilaterally for the abolition of a wages council; to empower the Employment Secretary to exclude individual firms from the scope of a wages council where there is evidence that voluntary collective bargaining arrangements are satisfactory; to allow a claim that 'recognised terms or conditions are not being observed' to be made by workers in wages council industries; and to empower wages councils to establish dispute proceedings for handling grievances raised by workers.

The Report was given detailed consideration by the trade unions at a specially convened post-Donovan Conference in March 1969 on the wages council sector.[6] The twenty-one unions attending were asked to comment on the Donovan proposals for wages councils which had already been described by the TUC's Acting General Secretary as 'timid'. The views of individual unions were also sought on seven suggestions from the TUC for improving trade union organisation in wages council industries:

(i) if wages councils are to continue to exist, is there a case for reducing the number and rationalising their field of operation?
(ii) abolishing the anonymity of wages council representation so that unions become signatories to Orders.
(iii) abolishing the system whereby the Minister appoints workers' sides and substituting selection by the union(s) concerned.
(iv) could wages councils themselves play a more positive role by actively encouraging trade union membership?
(v) including a provision that financial aid to unions to expand their membership in wages council industries should be through the Government's proposed Trade Union Development Scheme or through some other means.
(vi) the establishment of a trade union 'recruitment' committee in each group of industries to examine the problems, to set recruitment 'targets' and to co-ordinate organising activities.
(vii) agreements by unions on 'spheres of influence' and the withdrawal by unions from industries where their interest is marginal.

The TUC General Council also sought opinions on the desirability of extending the terms of reference of wages councils to enable them to deal with a much wider range of issues. Its consultative document mentioned dispute procedures, and pension, redundancy and productivity schemes as possible areas of interest. Co-operation with Economic Development Councils and Industrial Training Boards on matters

---

[6] See *Collective Bargaining and Trade Union Development in the Wages Council Sector* (TUC, 1969).

affecting efficient manpower utilisation, training and safety was suggested. If these proposals for expanding the role of wages councils were accepted, the TUC asked whether[7]

it might be desirable to propose also that each of the new councils should submit to the Minister an annual report on the progress made towards the objectives for which they were established. Such reports (which need not necessarily be unanimous) should cover the whole field of organisation and collective bargaining as well as matters arising from the direct exercise of their statutory powers.

No one reading this TUC document can be left in any doubt that here was the basis for a trade union led strategy against low pay. Yet the response in no way matched the possibilities which were opened up in the immediate post-Donovan era.

While a wide range of opinions were expressed at the conference the main lines of the debate were summarised by Jack Jones, the then leader of the Transport and General Workers Union:[8]

Two broad alternatives exist. Either the powers should be extended to widen their present limited coverage of wages and conditions, or they must be progressively abolished.

The T & G view was that

since Wages Councils do not represent an effective means of raising the standards of lower paid workers, they should be abolished.

The way forward, as the TGWU saw it, was on the basis of

the replacement of the Wages Council system with centralised national bargaining on minimum rates, such rates becoming an implied term of contract for all workers. *This would require a major campaign for trade union recruitment* (emphasis added).

In February 1970 the TUC General Council published a discussion document entitled *Low Pay*, which was based on a TUC staff and trade union research officers' working party report. It took account of the views expressed at the post-Donovan Conference and also considered the Government's Green Paper on *A National Minimum Wage* published by the DEP in May 1969.

The discussion document argued (para. 45) that the long-term aim of trade union policy '. . . should be to replace Wages Councils by voluntary collective bargaining machinery which is competent to tackle these problems effectively'. 'These problems' referred to low pay, efficiency, productivity, incomes structures and payments systems. However, it went on to argue:

[7] *ibid.* pp. 18–19.

[8] *ibid.*, p. 35.

At the moment the fact is that in the great majority of wages council industries their abolition would effectively remove what is an admittedly inadequate, but is nevertheless the only source of protection for the most vulnerable of working groups.

In conclusion it stated:

Wages Councils should be considered not so much as outmoded pieces of machinery to be abolished as and when effective alternatives are established – if ever this happens – but more as pieces of (albeit inadequate) negotiating machinery that need to be reformed and developed in stages towards the achievement of the desired voluntary machinery.

So we can see that trade union opinion was divided. However, what was characteristic of all unions, whether they were campaigning for abolition of wages councils or not, was the extraordinarily positive nature of their approach.

This positive approach was not to last. The trade unions saw the 1969 Wilson Government's White Paper *In Place of Strife* and the 1971 Industrial Relations Act as attacks on the right of free collective bargaining. The result was not only a souring of relations between unions and Government, but the unions beginning to equate any statutory involvement in industrial relations with an attack on free trade unionism. And, somewhat illogically, their rejection of any statutory involvement was not matched by any significant campaign to help the low-paid through free collective bargaining. From now on, with only a few exceptions like the G & M's initiative in appointing an officer with special responsibility for the wages council sector, the history of trade union action in the wages council sector becomes a negative one. The T & G promise of a major campaign for union recruitment never materialised. The proposal for a development fund was not heard of again. No effort was put into pushing each wages council into producing an annual report. No agreement was negotiated on 'spheres of influence'. Almost the only reform listed by the TUC post-Donovan Conference which was acted upon was the move to rationalise the number of wages councils – and this was organised by the Commission on Industrial Relations (a body which from early 1971 was boycotted by the trade union movement). By any standard, the performance over the past decade of attempting to make collective bargaining work in favour of the low-paid is a poor one, and this sorry record was established before unemployment rose to anywhere near its present total. But, as the TUC is proposing to initiate a series of conferences beginning in 1984 'to review progress on common objectives on low pay and working time', it is important to look at what might constitute a workable voluntary policy.

A voluntary approach again?

An idea of what constitutes the basis of an effective voluntary programme against low pay can be gained from the European papers prepared for the PSI Conference.[9] While Steve Winyard suggested that, *a priori*, the existence of a minimum wage system should lead to a greater equality in the distribution of earnings, his analysis showed that it was countries characterised by free collective bargaining which reported most progress in this respect. That this was so should not be too surprising. Barbara Wootton reminds us how in this country, and no doubt in others too, the determination of the current wage and salary structure is itself the product of social and economic forces rooted deep in history.[10] Moreover, what cannot be deduced from the figures is the distribution of earnings there would have been without the operation of a minimum wage. Yet it is important to look carefully at the main exceptions to Winyard's rule. The countries showing the least inequality in earnings are Norway and Sweden, but in both of them free collective bargaining is of a kind far removed from the way it operates in this country.

For a start, the trade unions in Norway and Sweden have played, and continue to play, a pivotal role in the share-out of that part of national income going to wages and salaries. Since the mid-1960s Sweden's trade unions have negotiated wage agreements containing special low-pay supplements; the aim of these supplements has been to increase the pay of the poorest workers, while at the same time decreasing the differentials between them and the rest of the working population. The Swedish LO has also endeavoured to obtain a common minimum wage policy across all agreements. And Sweden's trade unions' attack on low pay has been backed up by a progressive tax system, together with the payment of generous welfare benefits.

Even more impressive is the Norwegian record. The Norwegian LO now gives high priority to raising the income of the low-paid, and does so by negotiating special increases of up to 10 per cent for low-paid workers which are paid in addition to general wage increases. In 1980 it succeeded in obtaining a low-pay guarantee clause for that part of the private sector covered by negotiations between the LO and the Confederation of Employers (NAF). This agreement states that the average wage level in any firm should correspond to not less than 85 per cent of the average earnings of industrial workers. It has made a major difference to the distribution of earned income and, significantly, half the cost of the initial adjustment in wages is borne by the workers them-

[9] *Policies Against Low Pay, op. cit.*, especially chaps. 9 and 10.

[10] *op. cit.*

selves by a 1 per cent levy on earnings paid into a special fund. And, as in Sweden, this progressive trade union stance is backed by a fiscal and welfare policy which also aims at a greater equality of income.

The first question which needs to be posed to those advancing a voluntary strategy is whether the British trade unions can begin to match the actions of their Norwegian and Swedish colleagues. At the PSI Conference Lars Lundberg pointed out that Sweden differs from Britain in its industrial relations system; it is a small, fairly homogeneous country with a strong collective bargaining tradition. Here indeed are major variances, though discussions at the 1983 TUC Congress seemed to indicate a willingness to look again at the role of the TUC, taking greater account of the experience of its European counterparts. David Basnett, G & M's leader, for instance, reminded delegates of the German trade unions' stance for presenting their wage claims on a co-ordinated basis. The adoption of such an approach in Britain would lead to greater centralisation of decision-making and control, and would only happen if it were seen by the majority of trade unionists to be in their own interest. But once the trade union movement begins to build up a more central approach to wage bargaining, it ought to be possible to add on to it a similar low-pay strategy to that of the Norwegian and Swedish trade unions.

One of the actions of the promised 1984 conferences on low pay should be to consider whether the British trade union movement has the will to go down this road or not. A test of its will will be its preparedness to negotiate a levy system similar to that run by the Norwegian trade unions, to help finance a low-pay guarantee policy in this country.

A policy on pay deals

At the same time, the trade unions can begin discussions on whether the establishment of a minimum wage – either on a voluntary or a statutory basis – will be backed by a TUC stance disapproving of those wage claims which attempt to re-establish differentials. As the CPSA put it in its evidence to the TUC discussion document, *Low Pay* (p. 5):

A public declaration (by the TUC) to the effect that negotiators seeking the 'restoration of differentials' consequent to a statutory NMW would not receive TUC support, would have a significant effect on collective bargaining – not simply in terms of exhortation to bargainers but in the influence on arbitrators and mediators.

Individual groups of unions should also start discussions on whether they can begin implementing a minimum wage target within their field of collective bargaining. This would entail higher-paid workers forgoing part of the wage increase they might have expected in favour of a larger increase to those towards the bottom of the earnings pile. One such approach has already been put forward by the Council of Civil Service Unions in its evidence to the Megaw Inquiry.[11] Here the Council argued for a £85.00 a week minimum wage as part of its negotiating position and went on to state (p. 34) that it was:

> well aware that any programme to tackle low pay would raise practical problems, some of which would be acute. Nevertheless, we do not foresee any insoluble problems given a willingness, on the part of the Council's unions, to limit improvements under this programme to the low paid and to accept some overall compression of differentials.

A TUC policy aimed at preventing the re-establishment of differentials must be placed within a wider strategy of industrial regeneration. Collective bargaining, then, would not only be concerned with the total level of money wages and its distribution, but also with the total level of investment in the economy and with the skill levels workers will need if industries are to capitalise fully on the new investment.

There is a need for three further and by no means unimportant commitments. The first is to establish a development fund. It needs to be accepted by the entire trade union movement just how expensive it is to recruit members amongst low-paid workers. They are often to be found in establishments employing small numbers of people, and their job turnover appears to be substantially above that of other groups of workers. Clearly an intensive recruitment campaign over a long period of time will be expensive, and the cost should be shared throughout the trade union movement. The Government should also contribute and the fund should gain the support of all the major political parties. The 1964–70 Labour Government made an offer of financial support for this purpose and Liberal spokesmen have commented along similar lines. Moreover, the Conservative Government has legislated to provide public money to finance postal ballots within trade unions. Before low-paid workers are going to enjoy the privilege of voting, they need to be brought within the trade union movement.

However, a development fund by itself will not be effective in making a major difference to the recruitment of the low-paid. The idea of a development fund needs to be set within a wider campaign. In consultation with the unions concerned, the TUC should set recruitment targets for each of the main industrial occupations in which low-paid workers are to be found. It should decide spheres of influence and seek the withdrawal of unions from industries where they do not command majority standing. The allocation of monies from the fund should be determined by whether the union (a) is actively recruiting in

[11] Details in Council of Civil Service Unions, *The Bulletin*, Vol. 2, no. 1, 1982.

industries where it has been set targets and (b) has withdrawn from those industries where it has only marginal interests and where another union is seen as the main recruiting agent. The TUC should also monitor how quickly individual unions are achieving their recruitment targets.

Thirdly, the trade union movement should produce annual reports on the distribution of earnings. It appears that the TUC will not now continue to produce its annual economic statement or, if it does, it will be an exercise on a much reduced scale. The reason for this change is the growing realisation amongst trade unionists that there is little point in producing an alternative to the Government's economic policy if that Government has no interest in discussing the results. An annual report on the distribution of earnings – containing as it would a detailed look at the earnings of those at the lower end, together with the effect collective bargaining was beginning to have on the shape of the distribution – should take the place of the annual economic review. If the trade union commitment is present, this report will command the same prestige and resources as the economic review gained, and will thereby signify a change within the TUC in the whole emphasis of its work.

Conclusion

While this chapter has posed a voluntary policy as an alternative to a statutory one, it is possible to view them as twin parts of a single strategy. Such an approach becomes a more obvious course if the introduction of a minimum wage follows the lines suggested in this book. The NMW is set at a lower level than is currently demanded, but this level becomes the floor from which trade unions through collective bargaining seek to improve still further the living standards of the low-paid. This dual approach has been suggested over the years by Hugh Clegg.[12] The real test for the unions, however, is whether collective bargaining can perform for the low-paid markedly better than it has done in the past. As we have seen in this chapter, the trade union movement was slow to begin developing its own policy to combat low pay, and in the wages council sector – where the greatest number of the low-paid are employed – the unions failed utterly to respond to the challenge. The outlines of an effective voluntary policy have been drawn here. While it remains to be seen if the unions have both the idealism and the will with which to respond, there is no need to wait for the outcome of the next election before they open up their own discussions on whether or not a voluntary policy is workable. Indeed, it is crucial for this question to be answered during the next few years. If it is

[12] See for example *The Times*, 28 March 1967, and *Low Pay Review*, Low Pay Unit, 1982.

found to be viable, the low-paid will not have to wait for a centre-left radical majority in Parliament before gaining an improvement in their position. And if a voluntary policy is not a workable proposition, it is important that the early part of a new Parliament in which centre-left radicals have a majority is not paralysed while the trade unions *begin* a debate on offering a voluntary strategy.

9 Fiscal Changes

A review of the changing impact of direct taxation on households of different income levels over the past three decades has been given in Chapters 1 and 2. There we saw the extent to which the tax burden has shifted both vertically, on to tax payers with lower and lower incomes, and horizontally, on to tax payers with children. This chapter looks at the measures needed to raise the tax threshold, while at the same time helping to fund a major reduction in the rate of tax, particularly for those on low incomes. Three measures are discussed to bring most income into tax: placing a cash ceiling on what are called the non-structural tax benefits, allowing these tax benefits at the standard rate of tax only, and limiting the tax subsidy provided for company welfare benefits. A reversion to the former exemption scheme is also proposed. The chapter begins, however, with an explanation of how the structure of our income tax system militates against the piecemeal implementation of reforms aimed at helping the low-paid.

Raising the tax threshold
The reason why it is so costly to raise the tax threshold to any appreciable extent is because of the role played by what are called the personal allowances. These are awarded according to the status of the tax payer: there are the single and married person's tax allowances, the wife's earned income relief, and a number of other, less important allowances. Each of these allowances undertakes two functions in the tax system: it exempts a certain level of income from tax, but it also builds a gradation into the whole direct system of taxation. The only way to raise the tax threshold is to increase one or more of the personal allowances, but such a move has two major drawbacks. In the first place, any increase in the personal allowances fails to distinguish between those tax payers with children and those who are childless, and it is those tax payers with children for whom the tax threshold has fallen fastest in recent years. But the second disadvantage in operating on the personal allowances is that an increase in the allowances, in order to raise the tax threshold, not only helps those at the bottom of the income pile, but all other income tax payers as well. The financial barrier to bringing about a major shift in the incidence of taxation under the present tax structure can be seen by costing the raising of the threshold to the Council of Europe 'decency threshold' as regards income of 68 per cent of average

earnings. The cost of raising the threshold for all taxpayers is put at about £16bn.[1]

The falling tax threshold, particularly during the last couple of decades, has had a two-fold effect on the low-paid. It has meant that tax is raised on earned income which is below what the State defines as the poverty line. Moreover, for some taxpayers on the borders of poverty, the imposition of income tax and national insurance contributions pushes their net income below the supplementary benefit poverty line. Richard Berthoud has calculated, for example, that in 1975 6 per cent of the working poor would have had incomes above the supplementary benefit level if they had not been called upon to pay national insurance contributions, 11 per cent if they had paid no tax, and 14 per cent if they had paid neither.[2]

To raise the tax threshold, as well to cut the rates of tax, involves such expense that it can be embarked upon only in conjunction with a major overhaul of the structure of direct taxation. In practice, this means reforming the whole system of tax allowances which are best described now as constituting a 'tax benefit welfare State'. Four reforms need to go on to the agenda.

(a) *Tax allowances at the standard rate only*. Because tax allowances are set against the tax payer's marginal income, the tax benefit welfare State works in favour of those on higher incomes. Not only do those higher up the income scale have the ability to capitalise on the whole system but, ironically, the higher the income of the tax payer, the greater is the value of each of the tax allowances. An immediate reform can be achieved by allowing tax allowances at the standard rate only. This would leave the whole range of tax benefits intact, but as these benefits could be claimed only at whatever the standard rate of tax is, the value of benefits would become uniform irrespective of the taxpayer's income.

(b) *Cash ceiling on tax benefits*. The second reform entails a placing of cash ceilings on all but the personal tax allowances. Since the 1974–9 Labour Government first began to operate cash ceilings on the traditional welfare State, we have become aware of how effective this policy is in curtailing some areas of public expenditure. A similar policy should be operated on each of the non-personal tax benefits, including mortgage interest and life assurance relief.

---

[1] *House of Commons Hansard*, 11 July 1983, 251.

[2] See R. Berthoud and Joan C. Brown with Steven Cooper, *Poverty and the Development of Anti-Poverty Policy in the UK* (Heinemann, 1981) p. 44.

The need for such a policy is obvious when we look at how expenditure has grown in just one area of the tax benefit welfare State, compared with the traditional welfare State. If expenditure on social security over the period from 1960–61 to 1982–3 is revalued at constant prices, and a similar exercise is carried out for the tax benefit paid in mortgage interest relief, we find that social security expenditure had risen in 1982–3 by 241 per cent, while the value of the mortgage tax relief had increased by 368 per cent.

How a policy of cash ceilings on the tax benefit welfare State will work can be seen if mortgage tax relief is taken as an example. The proposal is that the current expenditure of this relief should be taken as a cash ceiling. In other words, if this policy was operating in 1982–3, a cash ceiling of £2.85bn would be put on the financing of mortgage interest relief. The building societies would be told that this was the total sum available for tax relief and that they should share this sum among those tax payers claiming relief. As a policy of operating tax relief at the standard rate only would also be in operation, the administration of the new scheme by the building societies would be simplified. The societies would have to estimate the number of net additional borrowers each year and how that tax benefit was to be spread amongst them. The societies currently operate a standard deduction scheme for savers, whereby they automatically deduct and pay the Government the standard rate of tax on interest accruing on the savings of each of their shareholders. A cash ceiling limit on the tax benefit welfare State would operate a not too dissimilar policy but in reverse. Paying each mortgagee the same sum relative to the size of his mortgage would not only be an egalitarian measure, but one which would also be easy to operate.

The extent of the revenue which would be gained by operating this cash ceiling policy on tax benefits can be seen from the following example. This looks at four tax benefits; mortgage interest relief, retirement annuity relief for the self-employed, and tax relief on life assurance premiums and pension scheme contributions. Table 9.1 lists, first, the estimated revenue costs of granting these four tax benefits in each financial year since 1975/6. It then calculates from these data the additional cost each year of allowing the tax benefit to rise above the 1975/6 ceiling. From these figures we can see that, to take mortgage interest relief again, the additional cost over and above the 1975/6 level is £4,565m. The total additional revenue cost for all four tax benefits stands in 1982/3 at £8,640m.

(c) *Paying for company welfare*. The third reform is to limit the growing expenditure on company welfare. As with other tax allowances or benefits, this area of welfare has grown significantly in recent years and,

96 *The Minimum Wage*

Table 9.1 (A) *Estimated revenue cost of various income tax reliefs (£m)*(a)

	1975/76	1976/77	1977/78	1978/79	1979/80	1980/81	1981/82	1982/83
Life assurance premiums	190	225	235	240	435	535	520	575
Mortgage interest relief etc	895	1,090	1,040	1,110	1,450	1,960	2,030	2,150
Pension schemes(b)	400	450	450	500	550	600	1,000	1,100
Retirement annuity relief for the self-employed	50	60	65	70	110	135	310	390

(B) *Increases since 1975/76 (£m)*

	1976/77	1977/78	1978/79	1979/80	1980/81	1981/82	1982/83	Total
Life assurance premiums	35	45	50	245	345	330	385	1,435
Mortgage interest relief etc	195	145	215	555	1,065	1,135	1,255	4,565
Pension schemes	50	50	100	150	200	600	700	1,850
Retirement annuity relief for the self-employed	10	15	20	60	85	260	340	790

Notes (a) All figures rounded to nearest £5m or £10m as appropriate.
(b) Rough approximations only.
Sources: The Government's Expenditure Plans 1983/4 to 1985/6, Cmnd 8789 – II, table 4.7.
House of Commons *Hansard* 18/4/83, 49 W; 8/3/83, 338 W; 2/11/79, 693 W; 14/1/81, 546 W.
House of Lords *Hansard* 25/1/79, 1730.
Inland Revenue Statistics 1982, table 1.6.

as we saw in Chapter 3, because it benefits most those on higher incomes, it increases rather than diminishes inequality and living standards. At the present time, the welfare expenditure of companies is deducted from a company's gross income, thereby reducing its tax liability. Some monies which would otherwise go to the Exchequer are re-directed into the pockets of employees, particularly higher-paid employees. There is a case for ruling that such expenditure should be made from the company's income after tax has been paid. In a free society companies should be allowed to develop their own systems of welfare, but other tax payers should not be expected to subsidise it, as they currently do. Moreover, the 'income' derived from such benefits must be valued accurately and be counted as part of individual taxable income.

(d) *An exemption scheme*. The fourth suggested reform is one which will take longer to implement and will need further discussion. It is to revert to the exemption scheme which operated in the income tax system up to 1920, the outline of which was given in *To Him Who Hath*.[3] Here it is only necessary to sketch in the broad outlines of the reform.

The proposal is that the personal allowances should be replaced by a specific 'exemption limit'. The exemption limit would ensure that incomes below this level were excluded from tax altogether, but those earning more than the limit would be assessed for tax on every £1 they earn. However, the reform cannot be one of reverting simply to the pre-1920s scheme. The problem with an exemption expressed as a maximum level of income beyond which an individual's income becomes taxable is that it carries with it a dramatically high marginal rate of tax as income moves above the limit. For example, if the exemption limit is put at £1,000, then, as a tax payer's income moves to £1,001, the whole of his income becomes liable to tax. One way of overcoming this drawback is to introduce a 'vanishing exemption' which diminishes in value as income rises, but is not withdrawn abruptly at any single cross-over point. Such a system would ensure a smooth withdrawal of the exemption as income rises, while at the same time ensuring that tax payers were not faced with a large jump in their marginal rates of tax.

To Him Who Hath gave the following notional figures for such a vanishing exemption scheme. It was suggested that income up to, say, a maximum of £1,000 would qualify for 100 per cent exemption. On income above this level, however, the value of exemption would be reduced by a third of the difference between gross income and the

[3] Frank Field, Chris Pond and Molly Meacher, *To Him who Hath* (Penguin 1977).

maximum exemption of £1,000. At £2,000, therefore, exemption would be two-thirds the full rate (£666.66) and at £3,000 the exemption would be at a third of the £1,000 exemption limit. On this model the exemption would be totally lost at incomes of £4,000 and above.

It must be stressed that these are only illustrative figures. The form of the final scheme would in part depend on the extent to which the withdrawal of the tax benefit welfare State was matched by a government's desire to reduce direct taxation, and the extent to which the tax reform contributed towards paying for the reform of the traditional welfare State. Moreover, it is possible to design a scheme by which the vanishing exemption operates much more gently, and over a much wider band of income. The effect, however, would be the same. No matter what kind of vanishing exemption scheme was finally adopted, the reversion to the pre-1920s system of income tax in this country would allow those on low incomes to be totally exempt from tax, while preventing any concessions to those on lower incomes accruing to tax payers further up the income scale. Moreover, once the exemption scheme was decided upon, the Government would also have the revenue to allow the introduction of many more bands of tax, and so introduce a truly progressive form of direct taxation. It would be possible, for example, to have income tax starting at 10p in the pound, and rising by units of 10p up to the top rate of tax.

A new social security tax

The first three of these reforms would finance a major lifting of the tax threshold and allow a government to cut the rates of tax. But poverty is also caused by the regressive nature of the national insurance contributory system. How best can this be reformed?

The major non-means-tested benefits, such as old-age pensions and unemployment and sick pay, are paid from the National Insurance Fund. The financing of this fund is highly regressive, with poorer workers paying a large part of their incomes in national insurance contributions. The contributory system works in the following way.

In the 1982–3 financial year a person earning less than £29.50 a week pays no national insurance contributions. Once that person's earnings reach this sum, the entire £29.50 becomes liable to a 9 per cent national insurance tax. Insurance contributions continue to be levied on income up to and including £220 a week. At this level what is known as a contribution ceiling comes into operation, whereby all additional income is ignored for national insurance contributory purposes. Above £220 a week, therefore, national insurance contributions in percentage terms begin to decline. So, while a married man with two children, earning an average wage in 1983–4, pays 8.4 per cent of gross income in

NI contributions, this percentage falls to 5.9, 2.4 and 1.2 per cent of gross income for those earning two, five and ten times average earnings.

For anyone concerned with increasing the net incomes of the low-paid, the National Insurance Fund is in urgent need of two major reforms. The first, which is important in its own right, does not concern the argument being developed here; consequently it needs only to be stated. As we saw in Chapter 3, large numbers of low-paid workers are made ineligible for national insurance benefits on account of their incomplete contribution records. They are now all too often made poor by this ineligibility. The first necessary reform, therefore, centres on loosening the eligibility rules for the whole range of national insurance benefits.

The second reform of crucial importance to the argument here is that the National Insurance Fund should be abolished and replaced by a social security and health budget. This would have three main sources of income: contributions from employers and employees and a general contribution from the Exchequer. The employers' contribution should continue along the present lines, with one change: the ceiling on contributions should be abolished so that the present proportional employers' tax continues to be paid on all incomes, no matter how high. The employees' contribution as such should be abolished, with the equivalent revenue being raised by levying a social security tax in addition to income tax. At the present time, employee contributions raise £9.1bn. The same sum could be raised by adding 10 pence on to the standard rate of income tax.[4] In addition, it is important to maintain an Exchequer contribution to the fund so that those who are not in work still help to finance part of the social security and health budget by way of their indirect taxation. Such a contribution is important in maintaining a person's right to benefits which have been earned. A second reform on the contributions front can occur when the income-tax changes proposed above are brought into effect: a graduated surcharge can then be levied on the different bands of income, with a smaller surcharge on each of the lower bands of income tax.

Conclusion

Poverty is caused not only by low wages but also by the tax and national insurance system. Income tax and national insurance contributions are collected on income far below the level defined by the State as the poverty line. If the reforms outlined in this chapter were implemented it would ensure that those on low earnings would be exempted from income tax and national insurance contributions altogether. The staged

---

[4] The age allowance would have to be adjusted to ensure that the majority of old age pensioners did not have to pay this increase.

reforms entail allowing tax benefits at the standard rates of tax only, placing a cash ceiling on all the non-structural tax benefits, and insisting that company welfare is paid out of gross rather than net income. Linked to these reforms is a suggestion for restructuring the National Insurance Fund. Such a package of measures would ensure that any increase in earnings resulting from the policies outlined in this book would not be cancelled out by demands from the Inland Revenue. Indeed, the reforms would allow a government to raise substantially the tax threshold, while at the same time cutting the rates of tax.

10 Reform of Equal Pay and Sex Discrimination Acts

Two decades ago reformers campaigned around the need to introduce equal pay and sex discrimination legislation. The information which was then to hand showed that a large proportion of low wage earners were women workers, and the expectation was that such measures would play an important part in raising their relative pay. This chapter looks at both of these acts, beginning with the Equal Pay Act. Its impact on female earnings is reviewed, before the discussion turns to an examination of why it has not been more successful in raising the pay of women workers. This is followed by a review of the Sex Discrimination Act, together with an examination of why this measure has failed to have greater impact. The final section looks at a programme of reform for both these measures.

Equal Pay Act
In introducing the Bill, the Employment Secretary, Barbara Castle, set out what she believed the measure would achieve. The Commons was told[1]

where other people have talked – lots of people have talked – we intend to make equal pay for equal work a reality, and, in doing so, to take women workers progressively out of the sweated labour class.

Mrs Castle went on to observe that while there were then 8.5 million women workers in employment 'some six million will be directly affected by this legislation, and that includes women who are engaged in what are traditionally "women's jobs" '. In addition, other women would be affected by what she called 'the halo effect'. Firms surveyed by her department reported that although none of their women workers qualified directly for equal pay 'they expected that they would have to increase their wages if increases were paid to women by other firms in the locality'.[2]

Events have not turned out in quite the way Mrs Castle foretold. The earnings data show a marked increase in the relative hourly earnings of

---

[1] *House of Commons Hansard*, 9 February 1970, 914.

[2] *ibid.*, 928.

women workers during the run-up period to the implementation of the act: from 63.1 per cent of male earnings in 1970 to 72.1 per cent five years later. But this progress has not been maintained. In 1977, for example, the relative hourly earnings of women workers rose from 75.1 per cent to only 75.5 per cent of those of men workers, an increase which led the Equal Opportunities Commission to comment that it saw a 'decreasing rate of progress towards equality' stemming from the operation of the Equal Pay Act.[3]

This note of caution turned to pessimism as earnings figures for subsequent years became available. In 1978 the EOC expressed 'alarm' at the current earnings trend, which showed women's gross hourly earnings declining to 73.9 per cent of men's gross hourly earnings in that year. A further decline in 1979 led it to declare that, taken together with all the available evidence, 'the effectiveness of the Equal Pay Act was now all but exhausted'.[4]

Why has the Equal Pay Act not been more effective? Part of the answer lies in the restrictions placed on the right to claim equal pay. First, a woman may only compare herself with a man employed by her employer or by a parent or related subsidiary company; she cannot make a claim based on a comparison with a man or woman doing similar work in any other firm. Second, in any tribunal hearing, the onus is on the woman to prove to the tribunal's satisfaction that she is engaged in 'like work', or in work regarded as equivalent under a job evaluation study. Presentation of a case in the first instance, and particularly from the position of being an employee, is often difficult. But if the claimant fails to satisfy the tribunal her claim will not be proceeded with further. And thirdly, a woman will have no grounds to claim at all if she is not engaged in 'like work' and her employer has not carried out a job evaluation exercise, and refuses to do so.

This last barrier will be partly removed by an amending Order to the Equal Pay Act which the Government was forced to introduce following a European Court ruling in July 1982 that the UK equal pay provisions did not meet with EEC requirements. The Order empowers a tribunal to initiate a job evaluation exercise in cases where it is satisfied that jobs may be of equal value. However, as with the original act, the new provisions are hedged with restrictions and in any case will not be fully effective before 1 January 1986. Technically, women should have been entitled to claim equal pay for work of equal value since 1976. However, no Order made under section 2 of the Act can take effect earlier than the date on which the Order was made. Hence,

[3] Equal Opportunities Commission, *Annual Report, 1977*, p. 5.

[4] EOC, *Annual Report, 1979*, p. 2.

under the (Amending) Regulations no equal value claim will be heard before 1 January 1984 and no tribunal will be able to award to a successful claimant the maximum compensation of two years' back pay until 1 January 1986. This situation has been contrasted unfavourably with the Government's provision in the Employment Act 1982 for retrospective compensation of 'closed shop victims' between 1974 and 1980.

The other major provision of the act has also turned out to have a limited jurisdiction. While the Central Arbitration Committee has a duty under the act to remove discrimination in collective agreements, this power is carefully circumscribed. The act states that 'the agreement may be referred, by any party to it or by the Secretary of State, to the Central Arbitration Committee'. The individual cannot make a reference directly to the CAC, although she can try to persuade her trade union or staff associates to do so, nor can a reference be made to the CAC by the EOC. The Secretary of State can make references to the CAC, so in theory, at least, an individual could make representations to the Secretary of State, requesting him to make a reference.

More important, however, is the fact that fewer women than men are covered by collective agreements, and the absence of formal published pay scales makes it more difficult than it otherwise might be in arguing that any particular rate of pay has discriminatary aspects attached to it. The disadvantage which flows from this is affecting some groups of women workers more rather than less as time goes on. A comparison between 1973 and 1978 NES data shows a slight increase in the numbers of manual women workers covered by no kind of collective agreement at all, be it a national or company agreement: from 28.3 to 29.1 per cent.[5]

Sex Discrimination Act

Working alongside the Equal Pay Act is the Sex Discrimination Act. When introducing this measure the then Home Secretary, Roy Jenkins, remarked that 'the unequal status of women in our society is a social evil of great antiquity'. He went on to comment:[6]

> The area of unequal treatment is vast. There is inequality in employment, in training and in related matters. There is inequality in educational opportunities. There is inequality in the facilities and services which women receive as members of the public.

Our concern here is only with those parts of the Sex Discrimination Act

---

[5] NES, 1973, tables 110 and 111, and NES, 1978, table 203 and 204.

[6] *House of Commons Hansard*, 26 March 1975, 511.

which relate to the employment conditions of women. Contractual matters, such as pay, are covered by the Equal Pay Act while the Sex Discrimination Act covers recruitment policies, promotion, firing, fringe benefits and other employment matters, other than contractual issues. One way of looking at these two acts is to consider the Equal Pay Act as attempting to change the structure of earnings, so that the pay of women is raised as a proportion of men's, while the Sex Discrimination Act, with its powers to forbid discrimination in education and training, allows the construction of ladders so that some women can escape from women's jobs into some of the better paid areas of male employment.

How well has the act worked in improving the status and conditions of women workers? As with the Equal Pay Act, the Sex Discrimination Act's impact has been limited. One reason for this is the number of areas excluded from its jurisdiction. Work in private households as au pairs, for example, is excluded, as is work carried out most of the time outside Great Britain. Similarly, employment in the Church or the armed forces is exempt, as are women working in active mines. While these may give rise to deeply held feelings of injustice in some women, most women would not be affected by these exemptions. This does not hold, however, for the exclusion of the act from work practices for employers who employ less than six people, or to complaints relating to retirement age or pensions (although following a ruling from the European Court of Justice in November 1983 it looks as though the British Government will have to tighten the law against sex discrimination). There are no comprehensive figures on the sex composition of employment in firms employing fewer than six people,[7] but what little information there is suggests that many more women than men are employed in small firms.[8]

In addition, there is a weakness in the Sex Discrimination Act's strategy which is similar to that in the legislation on equal pay. While men's employment is spread through the whole range of job opportunities, and no single industrial sector employs more than 10 per cent of the entire male workforce, women are found very largely in unskilled areas of work in the service and manufacturing industries. Six out of ten women workers are employed in the distributive trades, professional and scientific services and miscellaneous services (which cover laundries, catering, hairdressing). Thus even without the extra limitations imposed on comparisons by the Equal Pay Act and without the exemptions of the Sex Discrimination Act, it is difficult for legislation to

---

[7] *ibid.* 20 March 1980, 261.

[8] See 'Women's pay in informal payment systems,' *Employment Gazette*, April 1983, p. 141.

promote equality since, in many instances, women can only be compared with other women – in similarly reduced circumstances. While this points to the importance of reforms aimed at changing the distribution of earnings, there are other worthwhile changes to both acts which should be pursued.

Reforms

If a minimum wage is introduced at around £100.00 a week at 1982 prices, then the reforms about to be advocated for the Equal Pay Act will be less important in influencing the pay of women workers than will be the case if a minimum wage is set at £75.00 a week and is accompanied by a major injection of funds into the child benefit scheme. There are, in fact, five reforms being advanced by the EOC which are of particular importance.

The first concerns adding the concept of indirect discrimination to equal pay legislation. The Sex Discrimination Act contains the concepts of direct and indirect discrimination, with indirect discrimination being defined as the equal application of a condition or requirement to both men and women which has an unequal effect on one sex. An example here was the successful case brought against the Civil Service on the grounds that its recruitment of a certain category of employees between the ages of $17\frac{1}{2}$ and 28 years indirectly discriminated against many suitable women applicants for whom many of these years are child-bearing years. The Equal Pay Act does not include this indirect discrimination concept, and the EOC believes that its failure to deal with such indirect or disguised discrimination makes the British Equal Pay Act narrower than the requirements of EEC law.

A second reform concerns pay parity in instances where there is no comparable worker of the opposite sex. The Sex Discrimination Act does not require people treated less favourably because of their sex to find actual members of the opposite sex with whom to compare their treatment. The Equal Pay Act does. Because of the extent of job segregation in British industry it is often difficult for claimants to find a comparator for equal pay purposes. Amending the Equal Pay Act along the lines of the Sex Discrimination Act would extend its coverage to a wider group of women.

Over the past years there has been an increase in the numbers of part-time workers, and, while all too little is known about this group, the NES data show part-time work to be heavily concentrated amongst women workers. The tribunal decisions made under the Equal Pay Act indicate that most part-time women workers, attempting comparisons with the pay of full-time workers employed in the same work, fail to win their appeals. Amending the act so that part-time work was put on an equal hourly basis to full-time work would be of considerable help to the 40 per cent of women who work part-time.

As we saw earlier, it is only the two parties to a collective agreement, or the Secretary of State for Employment, who can refer a discriminatory provision in the agreement to the CAC. The EOC, which is given special responsibility for monitoring the Equal Pay Act, cannot make this reference, nor can an industrial tribunal. A small but worthwhile reform to the act would be to allow the CAC to review and, if necessary, strike out all direct or indirect aspects of discrimination found in collective agreements, pay structure or wage regulation orders referred to it, no matter who made the reference.

Under the present act a claimant may claim equal pay on a comparison with the rate being paid to a man doing the same or similar work, on the basis of a job evaluation scheme comparing the claimant's and a man's work, or via the CAC recognising discriminatory aspects of collective agreements when they are referred to it. The fifth, and perhaps the most fundamental, reform to the Equal Pay Act would be to allow equal pay claims to be based on equal value rather than like work value. Amending the act in this way would allow claims to be made by those who are doing work of equal value, but who cannot at the present time initiate proceedings because there is no man doing similar work, and there has been no job evaluation scheme. The idea would be to aim towards a situation where the CAC would attempt to establish the value of a job *per se* by taking into account the value of work which is for the most part now viewed as unrelated to the claimant.

There are far fewer reforms which it is worthwhile making to the Sex Discrimination Act. Shifting the burden of proof in sex discrimination cases would be a helpful reform – at least to claimants. At the present time the burden of proof in direct discrimination cases lies with the complainant. Direct evidence is rarely available, and where it exists it is usually in the possession of the employer. One reform would be for the onus of proof to be put on the employer – to prove that there was not direct discrimination. As small firms are exempt from the Sex Discrimination Act, and as women are more likely to be employed in small firms than are men workers, this exemption should be phased out (although the judgement of the European Court referred to earlier may force the Government to bring small firms within the scope of the act). Similarly, its scope should be extended to cover discrimination in death and retirement policies.

As well as reforming the Sex Discrimination Act, more use needs to be made of its influence, particularly within the education system. Again it is necessary to emphasise that the extent of job segregation in this country is not only based on the level of education reached by women – which on average is lower than that of men – but also on the subjects studied and the career aspirations of women which are set early on in the educational system. There is need for a major effort within our schools to begin changing the attitude of girls to the range of subjects which they can study, and the career prospects to which their qualifications based on these subjects will lead.

Conclusion

This will be a lengthy process, and it needs to be stressed now that the reforms suggested here may not have the major impact on women's relative earnings which some campaigners assert. According to one unpublished survey commissioned by the EOC, women's earnings in 1975, which stood at 62 per cent of male earnings, would have been increased to only 67 per cent had all forms of discrimination been abolished.[9] Once this report has been published it may be possible to dispute the analysis on which such conclusions have been based. But it does suggest that if the earnings of low-paid workers, who are overwhelmingly women workers, are to be improved, other measures outlined in this book need to be part of the strategy.

---

[9] The survey by A. Zabalza and Z. Tzannatos, 'Have women in Britain benefitted from equal pay?' quoted in Ian Hargreaves, 'Equal Pay: The Battle to Come', *Financial Times*, 30 March, 1983.

Conclusion

This study has argued the case for a national minimum wage in the following way. It has shown that a substantial number of those in poverty have been made poor by low pay. Using the FES data, we saw that over the past few years the numbers in poverty due to low wages have varied between 17 and 31 per cent. If the elderly are excluded from this calculation, the proportion rises to between 30 and 46 per cent. And these figures take no account of the way in which periods of low pay in a person's history can cause poverty today. Low-paid workers are most likely to be amongst the very poorest when they are unemployed and sick, and few low-paid workers are able to prevent themselves sinking into poverty when they retire.

The importance of low pay as a major cause of poverty was pushed back into political discussion in the mid-1960s. Since then, various policies have been initiated in an attempt to mitigate the effects of low pay. There has been much talk, but followed by far less action, on the need to reform the tax and benefit systems so as to prevent low-paid households being poor. Other initiatives have also been taken like the Equal Pay and Sex Discrimination Acts. While all these reforms have been substitutes for a direct attack on low pay, none of them has been successful in achieving its objectives. The reform which has yet to be tried is a national minimum wage.

Over the last year or so attitudes to this issue have been changing. Increasingly, important sections of the trade union and Labour movements have voiced their support for a national minimum wage. The Liberals have long advocated such a policy and, of all the centre-left radical groups, only the SDP remains outside this newly forming consensus.

There is, however, one aspect of this growing consensus which has been questioned in this book. The minimum wage target is now defined exclusively as two-thirds of average earnings. While a minimum wage set at such a level would have a major impact on the numbers of low-paid, it would not be set at a generous enough level to break the link between earnings and poverty. We have argued here that a minimum wage should be seen primarily as a measure to tackle family poverty. Once this is recognised as its aim, the role of child benefit has to be considered; but discussion of this has been completely lacking in public debate. There is a dramatic difference in the level at which a minimum wage needs to be set once it is assumed that part of the strategy is to introduce a fully developed system of child benefits.

Even if a minimum wage strategy is accompanied by the kind of increase in child benefits advocated in this book, raising wage levels by any appreciable amount, and especially at the present time, will have important economic repercussions, particularly on levels of employment and less so on inflation. Part of our argument has therefore been concerned to discuss the range of compensatory measures which need to be taken in conjunction with a national minimum wage initiative.

The proposal for a statutory minimum, rather than a voluntary one, may lead to strong objections from the trade union movement. These should be met by challenging the unions about their record over the past couple of decades. The trade union movement has been as strong in rhetoric as it has been weak in action in helping the low-paid. For nearly twenty years the TUC has excluded a statutory approach, emphasising in its place the role free collective bargaining has in helping the low-paid. An examination of the earnings figures shows that this approach has had no appreciable effect at all. As some trade unions may still argue that a voluntary approach must be given one more chance, this book has outlined the very minimum requirements if such an alternative is to be taken seriously.

A statutory minimum wage is posed therefore as an alternative to current policies – one which holds out the possibility of substantially raising the relative pay of workers at the bottom of the earnings pile. Because such a policy aims at improving the living standards of those currently on low pay, this book has also been concerned with other policies which will ensure that any increase in wages is not clawed back by taxation. As well as advocating a radical overhaul of the fiscal system, reforms are advocated to the Equal Pay and Sex Discrimination Acts.

Mention was made in the Introduction that this book grew out of PSI's international conference on minimum wage regulation. After its publication, it is intended that some aspects of the argument will be developed further in shorter publications (e.g. on the machinery for operating a minimum wage), and that these supplementary papers, together with the main findings of the conference, will be discussed at specially convened seminars. The aim is to look at the policies advocated in this book with participants from business and the trade union movement, together with representatives of consumer organisations, anti-poverty groups and the academic community. Centre-left radicals may well hold the balance of power in the next Parliament, and if so, it is necessary that the policies which they may adopt should have been thought out carefully during the two or three years before the next general election.

Appendix 1   *Calculations of the NMW level (April 1982)*

Calculations are for what a wage earner would need to earn in order to give him/her a gross income equivalent to the supplementary benefit level for a married couple with two children. The calculations are in two parts assuming: (a) no change in the level of child benefit and (b) child benefit equal to the additional benefit paid to the children of claimants drawing the higher rates of national insurance benefits.

The calculation of the supplementary benefit entitlement is divided into three stages:

(i) *the payment for two children*

Here the different scale rates for children have been averaged out to a single payment equal to £13.17. For two children the weekly supplementary benefit entitlement equals £26.35 (rounded to the nearest 5p).

Child benefit is deducted from supplementary benefit rates. Child benefit in 1982 stood at £5.25 a child, or £10.50 a week for two children. The total supplementary benefit entitlement for two children therefore equals £15.85p (£26.35 supplementary benefit entitlement minus £10.50 child benefit).

The second stage in the calculation for the children's entitlement is to assume that child benefit is raised to equal the additional rate paid to the children of higher-rate national insurance beneficiaries. This would give a child benefit equal to £12.95 a week for each child, the benefit for two children equalling £25.90. The supplementary benefit entitlement is therefore £26.35 supplementary benefit minus £25.90 child benefit, or a 45 pence weekly addition.

(ii) *The payment for a married couple*

Chapter 5 set out the reasons for using the long-term rate. For a married couple this stood at £47.35 a week.

(iii) *The rent payment*

Households on supplementary benefit are entitled to have their rent paid in full. The latest weekly rent payment figures are for local authority tenants in December 1981, when the average payment for non-pensionable households stood at £15.25.

Appendix 1

The supplementary benefit entitlement for a household, assuming no change in child benefit payments, equals

    £15.85 for two children
    £47.35 for a married couple
    £15.25 as the average rent payment
    ―――
    £78.45 total supplementary benefit entitlement.

The entitlement changes if it is assumed the child benefit is paid so that it equals the additional rate paid to the children of higher-rate national insurance beneficiaries.

    £ 0.45 for two children
    £47.35 for a married couple
    £15.25 for rent
    ―――
    £63.05 total supplementary benefit entitlement.

The gross income equivalent which a worker needs to earn to have a net pay packet of £78.45 is £102.20 a week. The figure for a net weekly income of £63.05 is £76.89.

Appendix 2   *The importance of the child benefit scheme*

While a generous system of child benefits affects the level at which the national minimum wage needs to be set if it is to break the link between earnings and poverty, it also has a major impact on the feasibility of introducing other welfare reforms which, together with action against low pay, begin to make up an anti-poverty programme. Given the importance of seeing action on low pay in relation to these other areas, this appendix briefly reviews the other advantages which stem from a fully developed system of child benefits.

The first is that, while many old people are trapped into poverty as soon as they retire, poverty is now found to a greater and greater extent amongst those groups of the population below retirement age. An increase in child benefit is the most immediate and effective means of tackling the problem of family poverty amongst those who work, and it does so in a way which increases rather than decreases the incentives to work.

Secondly, child benefit changes are also important as a means of maintaining tax equity. Since 1909, when child tax allowances were re-introduced, Chancellors have been able to maintain tax equity between childless tax payers and those with children by increasing child tax allowances at the same time as revising the other personal allowances. 1977 saw the phasing out of child tax allowances to coincide with the introduction of child benefits. With the final abolition of child tax allowances in 1980 (except for tax payers with dependent children overseas), child benefits took on a dual function. On the one hand, they have become a most effective way of channelling resources to families on low income. On the other hand, they now constitute the only mechanism by which Chancellors can increase the tax-free income of tax payers with children when making regular revisions in the level of tax-free income for other tax payers. Earlier in our discussions we looked at the extent to which the tax burden had moved against not only the low paid, but also tax payers with children (see Chapters 1 and 2). The introduction of a generous system of child benefits will play an important part in redressing this horizontal inequity in the tax system.

Thirdly, a generous system of child benefits will play a crucial part in transforming the welfare State into a system of benefits on which people can build by their own efforts, and not be penalised for so doing. Child benefits are at the present time tax-free and non-means-tested. This means they are kept in full by families in work, irrespective of the family's level of earnings. Any programme, particularly one which will be immensely expensive, will have to be implemented in stages. A big increase in child benefits will have an immediate and important effect on the activities of those families living on incomes near to the poverty line. For example, the ideal way of tackling poverty amongst single-parent families is the introduction of a single-parent family allowance. Yet the doubling of child benefits in real terms would bring about a significant reduction in the number of single parents depending on means-tested supplementary benefits. Some would have their incomes taken above the supplementary benefit poverty line and would therefore become ineligible. But other one-parent families, whose income was not brought up to the poverty line, might well decide that child benefit payments now provided enough of a launching pad to free them from means-tested benefit support, providing they were accompanied by the adequate provision of day-care facilities for their children. This would almost certainly be the case if a NMW was introduced, even at the lower level proposed in this book.

Fourthly, an adequate child benefit payment will increase the economic power and status of women in our society. Family poverty amongst the working poor is a characteristic of households with young children. While many families are sprung from poverty only by the advent of a second wage in the household, many mothers still prefer to remain at home when their children are very young. Adequate child benefits will increase their income as of right and should be linked to the introduction of a home responsibility allowance, (for which people caring for aged relatives would also be eligible) financed by the phasing out of the married man's tax allowance.[1]

---

[1] For details of this, see Frank Field, *Inequality in Britain*, op. cit., pp. 182–3.

Index

Abel-Smith, Brian, 25n., 26
absence from work, 9, 26, 27–8
Agricultural Wages Board, 52, 58
agriculture/farming, 61, 63, 77, 80
age, 57, 105
    of fathers, 73–4
arbitration system, 67–8 see also CAC
Atkinson, A.B., 30, 33, 41, 53
Attacking Poverty (SDP), 40, 45
Attlee Government, 83
au pairs, 104
Australia, 67–8

Basic Benefit (SDP), 46–7
Basnett, David, 89
Berthoud, Richard, 94
Beveridge proposals, 37–8
Bisset, Liz, 7n., 53
Black Report, 31–2
Booth, Charles, 51n., 52
Bosanquet, Nicholas, 30
box-making, 68
building societies, 95
Bulkley, M.E., 68

CAC, 103, 106
Callaghan Government, 14
Canada, 66
carers, 56, 113
Carter, Charles, 76n., 80
Castle, Barbara, 101
CBI, 64, 84
chain-making, 68
child benefit, 1, 2, 29, 37–8, 45, 49, 57–9, 60, 61, 71–4 *passim*, 81, 105, 108–13
    see also family allowances
CIR, 87
Civil Service, 105
    Council of, Unions, 90
Clegg, Hugh, 91
collective agreements, 18, 19, 20, 103, 106
collective bargaining, 3, 19, 82, 84–91, 109
company benefits, 36, 93, 95–6, 100
compensatory measures, 2, 49, 65, 69–70, 71–81, 109
Conservative policy, 16–24, 37, 39, 83, 90
construction, 20
Cooper, Lord, 83

cost of living, 13–14, 17–18, 24 see also inflation
costs, 37, 39, 72, 93–4, 95
    of children, 57–9
    of NMW, 2, 49, 60–61, 66, 69–72, 74–5, 77, 88–9
CPAG, 38, 39
CPSA, 89

day-care facilities, 113
'decency threshold', 7–9, 93
definitions, of low pay, 7, 14, 20–21, 53–4
    see also poverty
DHSS, 30, 32, 33
differentials, wage, 60, 65–7, 69, 70, 76, 81, 84, 88, 89–90
Dix, Bernard, 82, 83
Donovan Commission/Report, 84–5

earnings, 5, 7–12, 14–15, 20–21, 53–4, 82, 84, 88–9
    and poverty, 1, 2, 25–30, 51, 53–4, 56, 59, 61, 65, 74, 108, 112
    distribution, 7–12, 88, 90, 91, 105
    guarantee, 1, 75, 83–4, 88–9
    overtime, 47, 53
    -related supplement, 42, 43, 55
    replacement rate, 43–5
    women's, 9–12 *passim*, 26–7, 53, 61–3, 71–2, 83, 101–5, 107
    youth, 21–3, 66–7, 71–4 *passim*, 81
Eccles, Mary, 66, 73
Economic Development and Planning (TUC, 1963), 82
Economic Development Councils, 85
Clothing, 77
Economic Review (TUC, 1968), 83
education, 78–80, 103, 104, 106–7 see also training
EEC, 79, 102, 105
employers' associations, 84
employment, 1, 2, 18, 19, 22–3, 43–5, 47, 49, 64–9, 70, 71–6, 78, 81, 103–4, 109
    concentration, 9–10, 21, 61–4, 71, 84, 91, 101, 104, 105
    measures, 78
    part-time, 10, 22, 35, 105–6

women, 9–12, 22, 56, 61–4, 69, 71, 101–7
youth, 23, 65–8 *passim*, 72–3, 78–80
Employment Act (1980), 21, (1982), 103, Protection Act (1975), 18
Employment, Department of, 11, 73, 86
Employment, Secretary, 19–23 *passim*, 85, 101, 103, 106
EOC, 56, 102, 103, 105, 106, 107
Equal Pay Act, 3, 49, 72, 101–3, 104, 108, 109
  reform of, 105–6
Europe, Council of, 93
European Court, 102, 104, 106
European Social Charter, 7, 14
expenditure patterns, 14, 27

Fair Wages Resolution, 16, 18–20, 24
family allowances, 38, 39, 43, 57
FES, 1, 14, 26, 27–9, 36, 41, 108
Fiegehen, G.C., 27
FIS, 37, 38–9, 41–3, 45–7 *passim*, 53–4
Fisher, Alan, 82, 83
food costs, 13, 14
France, 67
fuel costs, 13, 18

G & M, 83, 87, 89
Germany, 89
GHS, 30, 31, 32, 56, 58
Government Actuary, 34, 35
government contracts, 18, 20
guarantee, wage, 75, 88, 89
Guardian, The, 66, 75

handicapped, 56
Heath, Edward, 39
Henley Centre for Forecasting, 69, 74
home responsibility allowance, 113
House of Commons Treasury and Civil Services Committee, 41–2
housing benefit, 46, 47, 59
Howell, Ralph, 36n., 42–3

IDS, 20, 32
IEA, 64
In Place of Strife (1969), 87
incentives to work, 2, 5, 36, 37, 42–5, 112
incomes policy, 20, 66, 71, 75–7, 81, 83
Industrial Relations Act (1971), 87
inflation, 2, 5, 12–18 *passim*, 48, 49, 66, 68, 71, 74–5, 76, 81, 84, 109
institutions, inmates of, 28
invalidity benefit, 57
investment policy, 71, 77–8, 80, 81, 90

Jenkins, Roy, 103
job
  evaluation, 102, 106
  segregation, 105, 106
  turnover, 33, 90
Jones, Jack, 55–6, 86

Labour Party policy, 2, 29, 37, 38, 83, 90, 94, 108
Lansley, P.S., 27
level of NMW, 1, 2, 7, 49, 51–9, 73, 91, 108–12 *passim*
levy *see* trade unions
Liberal Party, 2, 52, 90, 108
life assurance, 94–6 *passim*
living standards, 7–9, 12, 13, 14, 56, 70, 93
  of low-paid, 2, 3, 5, 12, 13, 14, 31, 33, 42–5, 49, 51–3, 91, 109
LO, 88–9
Longford, Lord, 37
low-paid, numbers of, 2, 7–10, 14, 24, 27–30, 38, 45, 47, 52, 61–4, 108
Low Pay, 86, 89
Low Pay Unit, 5, 14, 41
LPPI, 14, 17, 18
Lundberg, Lars, 89

MacDonald, Duncan, 67
MacLennan, Emma, 7n., 53
Macleod, Iain, 39
manpower policy, 71, 78–80, 86
manual workers, 9, 10, 21, 30–31, 34–5
Marquand, Judith, 82
Marshall, Alfred, 69
means-tested assistance, 37–43, 45–7, 113
  see also individual headings
Megaw Inquiry, 90
mortgage interest, 12, 17, 18, 94–6
Muellbauer, J., 14

NAF, 88
National Economic Development Council, 78
national insurance
  benefits, 26, 28, 34, 40, 42–5, 55, 57–9, 98–9, 110, 111
  contributions, 13, 16, 34, 41, 43, 47, 94, 98–9
  eligibility rules, 99
  Fund, 57, 98–9, 100
  threshold, 10, 98–9
National Minimum Wage, A (1969), 86
nationalised industries, 20
NBPI, 7, 53
NES, 7, 9, 11, 30, 57, 60, 103, 105
non-manual workers, 9, 21, 32, 34–5

Norway, 75, 88–9
NUPE, 76, 82

OECD, 66, 67
old age, 25, 33–6, 108, 112
OPCS, 32, 73
Ormerod, Paul, 69
overtime, 47, 53

part-time workers, 10, 22, 35, 105–6
pensions, 34–6, 98, 104
  schemes, 33–6; occupational, 33, 34–5
  tax relief, 12, 95–6
Piachaud, David, 13–14
Pinder, John, 76n., 80
Poor and the Poorest, The, 25, 26, 38
poverty, 1, 2, 5, 7, 25–47 *passim*, 54–9, 72, 74, 99, 108
  and low pay, 1, 2, 5, 7, 25–36, 51, 54, 61, 72, 74, 108
  and old age, 25, 33–6, 112
  and sickness, 31–3
  and unemployment, 30–31
  definition of, 7, 10, 25–6, 51–2, 54
  line, 26, 34, 38, 42, 51, 58, 94, 99, 113
  trap, 2, 37, 38, 39–45, 46–7
Poverty in the United Kingdom, 26
prices, 13–14, 17, 22, 30, 70, 74–5, 80 *see also* inflation; RPI
productivity, 70, 77–8, 80, 81, 84
professional workers, 30, 31, 35
profit margins, 75, 77
PSI conference, 1, 2, 7, 9, 21, 25, 53, 66–7, 75, 88, 89, 109

Rathbone, Eleanor, 38, 57
rent, 18, 43, 55, 58–9
  and rate rebates, 37, 38, 39, 43, 46, 47, 58–9, 110–11
replacement rate, 43–5
research findings, 5, 21, 30, 66–70, 72–3
retail sector, 22, 23, 61
retirement, 104, 106, 108, 112
  annuity tax relief, 95–6
Rodgers, Barbara, 2
Rowntree, B. Seebohm, 10n., 25, 26, 51–2
Royal Commission on Distribution of Income and Wealth, 13, 27
Royal Commission on Industrial Relations, 84–5
RPI, 12, 13–14, 17–18, 24

safety, 86
Sandavall, Véronique, 67
savings, 33, 55
Schedule 11, 16, 18, 20–21, 24

school leaving age, 78, 80
  meals, free, 37, 38, 39, 45, 46
SDP, 2, 37, 40, 45–7, 108
services, personal, 30, 61–3, 104
Sex Discrimination Act, 3, 49, 103–5, 106, 108, 109
  reform of, 106
sick pay, 32–3, 55, 57, 98
  schemes, 32–3
sickness, 26, 28, 31–3, 108
single-parent families, 56, 113
single persons, 13, 16–17, 34, 56
size
  of family, 14, 39, 51, 52–3, 58
  of firm, 35, 90, 104, 106
skills, 77–80, 90
SMIC, 67
Smith, D., 27
Social Trends, 40
Society of Civil and Public Servants, 9
staging, of NMW, 65, 71–2, 81, 113
statutory minimum wage rates, 9, 20, 22–3, 52–3, 65, 66–70, 73
structural changes, in industry, 78
subsidies, price, 75
supplementary benefit, 1, 7, 26, 27–9, 34, 43, 54–7, 59, 110–11, 113
  and NMW, 1, 54–6, 110–11
Sweating Committee, 18
Sweden, 88–9

T & G, 55, 86, 87
tailoring, 68
Tawney, R.H., 68–9
taxation, 5, 16–17, 39–42, 43, 46–8, 57, 88, 89, 93–100, 109, 112
  allowances, 12, 39, 93–7, 112, 113
  and children, 12–13, 16–17, 24, 39, 93, 112
  benefits, 12, 45, 93, 94–8, 100
  burden, 3, 12–13, 15–17, 23–4, 93, 112
  exemption, 97–8
  rates, 12–13, 38, 39, 40–42, 47, 49, 93, 94, 97–100 *passim*
  rebates, 43, 55
  reforms, 3, 94–100, 108
  reliefs, 43, 94–6
  social security, 98–9
  threshold, 12–13, 38, 39, 41, 47, 49, 93–4, 98, 100
To Him Who Hath, 97
Townsend, Peter, 25n., 26
trade unions, 2, 3, 5, 7, 19–20, 49, 54, 69, 75–6, 82–92, 108, 109
  development fund, 85, 87, 90–91

levy, 75, 77–8, 89
membership, 19, 20, 85, 86, 87, 90–91
spheres of influence, 85, 87, 90
trades boards, 9, 52
training, 78–80, 86, 103, 104
  Industrial – Boards, 85
TUC, 5, 53, 54, 76, 82, 83, 84–7, 89, 90, 91, 109
  conference (1969), 85, 86–7

unemployment, 5, 12, 23, 26, 27, 28, 30–31, 33, 42–5, 60, 61, 64, 65, 66–9, 70, 73, 83, 87, 108
  benefits, 42–5, 55, 57, 98
  distribution of, 30
  trap, 42–5, 47
  youth, 23, 66–7, 72
United States, 66–7, 70, 73
  Minimum Wage Study Commission, 66–7

VAT, 17

wage settlements, 16, 21–3, 24, 64, 88, 89–91

Wages Councils, 9–10, 21–3, 24, 65, 68, 84–9, 91
  Inspectorate, 9
  orders, 9, 20, 22–3, 65, 68–9
Warwick University Industrial Relations Unit, 21
why work syndrome, 36, 42–5
widows benefit, 57
Wilson Government, 14, 87
Winyard, Steve, 7n., 88
women, 9–12, 22, 31, 32, 33, 35, 53, 56, 60, 61–4, 69, 71, 101–7, 113
  earnings of, 9–12 *passim*, 26–7, 53, 61–3, 71–2, 83, 101–5, 107
  married, 26, 27, 32, 56
Wootton, Barbara, 52–3, 54, 58, 65, 88
World War, First, 9
  Second, 18, 25, 82

York, 25, 52
young workers, 9, 21–3, 65, 66–7, 72, 78–80
  minimum wage rate, 66–7, 71, 72, 73–4, 81
Youth Opportunities Scheme, 78
Youth Training Scheme, 78–80

DATE DUE			
NOV 17 '87			
DEC 1 '87			
JAN 19 '88			
OCT 25 '88			
NOV 9 '98			

PRINTED IN U.S.A.